HOW TO
BRING IN NEW
PARTNERS

A GUIDE FOR FIRMS AND FUTURE PARTNERS

ALSO BY MARC ROSENBERG

The Role of the Managing Partner
CPA Firm Staff: Managing Your #1 Asset
CPA Firm Partner Compensation: The Art and Science
CPA Firm Partner Retirement/Buyout Plans
CPA Firm Growth: Keys to Practice Development
CPA Firm Mergers: Your Complete Guide
How CPA Firms Work: The Business of Public Accounting
CPA Firm Retreats: The Do-It-Yourself Guide
CPA Firm Management & Governance
CPA Firm Succession Planning: A Perfect Storm
Strategic Planning and Goal Setting for Results
CPA Firm Partner Agreement Essentials
How to Operate a Compensation Committee
What Really *Makes CPA Firms Profitable?*
Effective Partner Relations and Communications

For more information or to order additional titles visit:
rosenbergassoc.com

Connect with Marc:
marc@rosenbergassoc.com

HOW TO
BRING IN NEW
PARTNERS

A GUIDE FOR FIRMS AND FUTURE PARTNERS

MARC ROSENBERG, CPA

ROSENBERG RAMPE
Practice Management

CONTENTS

Foreword

Succession planning eventually rises to the top of every retirement-minded partner's to-do list. For some, the process starts early; for others it's the last thing they want to think about, so it's put off until there's almost no time left. In both cases, the need to bring new talent into the ownership ranks is critical for a CPA firm to remain independent.

Sole practitioners bringing in their second partner often have no idea where to start. Multipartner firms that haven't admitted a new partner in a decade or more probably know that the way they did it last time won't work this time.

In 2009, Marc wrote his first book about bringing in new partners at public accounting firms. The result was a short 58-page guide that assisted over 1,500 firms in their quest to admit owners in a way that worked for the practice and the individuals.

Today, Marc uses his latest insights to comprehensively address every issue in adding owners to your firm in this newly expanded book, *How to Bring in New Partners: A Guide for Firms and Future Partners.*

In my work with Marc, I have seen firsthand his ability to guide firms to making decisions that have a positive impact on their long-term success. This book will guide you as if Marc were by your side.

Kristen Rampe, CPA
Rampe Consulting

1

Introduction

Accounting firms worldwide are dealing with an enormously difficult challenge today—one that has topped every firm's list of critical issues since the turn of the century and will continue to be a high priority for years to come. The vast majority of firms struggle with it. Failure to solve it causes hundreds of firms to merge out of existence every year.

The "it" is, of course, succession planning, with difficulties rooted in a perfect storm of causes:

- The huge number of baby boomer partners nearing or reaching retirement age, coupled with ...

- An acute shortage of younger people with the desire and the skills to succeed them, accompanied by ...

- CPA firms' historical weakness at retaining staff and developing them into leaders and future partners. Evidence of this is the fact that 80% of first-generation firms never make it to the second.

How to Bring in New Partners:
One of the Hottest Issues at CPA Firms Today

Succession planning challenges are causing firms to scrutinize more than ever before their methodology for bringing in new partners. From developing staff into leaders and partners to revising financial models for new partner buy-ins and buyouts for retiring partners to transitioning clients to successor partners, these long-neglected and somewhat dysfunctional issues are increasingly being brought to the front burner.

Compounding the challenge of bringing in new partners is the simple fact that few firms have *recent* experience in doing so. Indeed, there are thousands of firms that have never made *anyone* a new partner. These firms are grasping at straws trying to figure out a coherent plan for bringing in new partners that is a win-win for both the existing partners and the new ones.

Undoing Firms' Archaic Practices

If any of the characterizations below sound familiar, you need to re-engineer your approach to bringing in new partners:

1. **No handholding**. "Older" partners often feel they earned their partnerships the old-fashioned way, through hard work and perseverance, without anyone "holding their hand." They expect nothing less from today's young people. Partners' attitudes all too often seem like this: "We want to wait until the staff show us that they have the right stuff. Staff must come to us *first* and *tell* us they want to be a partner. Then and only then will we step in and show them the way."

    Many of today's older partners have a tough time accepting that this attitude has shifted in the past 10 to 20 years. Hard work, ambition and perseverance are still important. But today, it's also important to show young people the way by mentoring them and *proactively* helping them develop, all of which must begin years before a staff member is ready to be a partner.

2. **Lack of formalized criteria for making partner.** One practice that greatly hinders leadership development is firms' reluctance to

formalize and communicate to their staff written criteria for making partner. How can staff be expected to aspire to become partners if they don't know what it *takes* to become a partner and what it *means* to be a partner?

3. **Widely varying criteria for making partner.** Somewhat related to the point above, firms today have a vast range of criteria for making partner, especially in the area of bringing in business. For example, some firms believe that in order to be a partner, a person has to be an accomplished business-getter; these firms will rarely promote anyone to partner without this attribute. On the other hand, some firms have little or no requirements to bring in business to qualify for a partnership. There is no consensus on this in the CPA firm industry, especially at firms under $15M in revenue.

4. **Inconsistencies in the system.** Many firms make new partners so infrequently that every time they bring in a new owner they change the system for buying into the firm. This makes for inconsistent and often incomprehensible methods for bringing in new partners.

5. **Prohibitive new partner buy-ins.** Years ago, buy-ins were huge: several hundred thousand dollars. Today's new partners have neither the financial resources nor the willingness to pay these astronomical sums. Today, well over 90% of firms—of all sizes—establish a new partner buy-in that is smaller and more affordable than in the past.

6. **Reluctance to use the non-equity partner position.** In years past, for the most part, there was only one class of partner: an equity partner. Many firms made the mistake of promoting directly to equity partner staff who lacked important talents and experience, primarily in business development and leadership skills, to function as business owners. Today, CPA firms are making increasing use of a second tier of partner, the *non-equity* partner. As a result, they have raised the bar for what it takes to become an equity partner.

Where Leadership Development Starts

No matter which thorny practice management issues I've been called in to address over more than 20 years of consulting, one consistent observation keeps coming across loud and clear: CPA firm partners *really* love their jobs!

Do partners come to work every morning grinning from ear to ear and shouting to all who will listen how happy they are? Of course not. But when they sit back and think about how fortunate they are to be a partner in their firm, they feel very satisfied. Opportunities to help clients abound. Every day presents a new challenge—and CPAs love solving problems. They enjoy the freedom and flexibility of being business owners. And they love making more money than they ever dreamed of. Partners in local firms earn, on average, $300,000 to $800,000 a year.

If today's young people, from students pondering the selection of a college major to staff already working at CPA firms, realized how truly fantastic a job it is to be a partner in a CPA firm, our profession's succession planning challenge would be more easily solved.

You would think that partners would enthusiastically communicate their love of the game to their staff. But they don't.

You would think that staff would be dreaming of the day when they succeed in becoming partners. But they don't because their firm is probably not telling them what it means to be a partner and what it takes to become one.

CPA Firms Are Too Secretive

It's positively maddening that CPA firms tend to be very secretive about two things that would excite young people to no end:

CPA partners make lots of money. A common belief among "older" partners is that money doesn't mean much to young people. This couldn't be farther from the truth. Throughout my consulting career of more than 20 years, survey after survey consistently shows that compensation is either #1 or #2 on the list of what's important to staff.

4

Recent results of the annual Rosenberg MAP Survey show average compensation of local CPA firm partners to be $470,000. I'm quite sure that the compensation of a CPA partner is higher than that of 95% of all other jobs.

Given the importance of compensation to staff, and the fact that CPA firm partners make lots of money, you would think that partners would communicate this motivating fact loud and clear to staff. But they don't.

Partners tend to feel that their compensation is confidential. Or that it's nobody's business to know what they earn. Perhaps they feel that telling the staff what partners earn, on average, would make them appear to be flaunting it—greedy, conceited, overly materialistic. But there are ways to communicate their lucrative compensation without making partners or staff uncomfortable.

What it takes to make partner. We have interviewed hundreds of CPA firm staff. We ask them these questions:

- Do you know what it takes to make partner?
- Has anyone in the firm had a serious discussion with you about your future at the firm?
- Has anyone asked you if you want to be a partner?
- Do you *want* to be a partner?
- If you don't want to be a partner, why not?

You would think firms would routinely have this conversation with their staff, especially those with partner potential. But they don't.

Partners have a tendency to keep lots of things secret that should be open, formalized and stated in writing, including the firm's criteria for making partner. The main explanation we hear for *not* documenting such information in writing is concern that it could backfire. Partners fear that staff will prematurely march into the MP's office waving this document, insisting that they've fulfilled all the criteria for making partner and demanding a date when the coronation will take place.

So, many firms purposely don't formalize their criteria for partner. They reason that being less formal gives them more wiggle room to use their subjective judgment (or bias) in deciding who to make partner.

But this secrecy creates problems in leadership development. If talented staff don't know what it takes to become partner and have minimal conversations with partners on the subject, the firm's ability to retain great staff is hindered considerably.

What a disconnect! I constantly hear partners complain about today's young people. Their common refrain: "These days staff don't want to be partner." My experience in interviewing and surveying hundreds of staff is that they may *say* they don't want to be a partner, but the real obstacle is that they simply don't know what it takes to *become* a partner, what it *means* to be a partner and how great a job it really is.

Who This Book Is Written For

There are two audiences for this book:

1. **CPA firms** seeking guidance on how to develop staff into partner candidates who eventually are promoted to partner. This is from two perspectives:

    - Structuring the financial and operating aspects of making someone a partner. We address the buy-in, ownership percentage, capital, voting, new partner compensation, duties of the new partner, equity vs. non-equity partners, partner buyout and partner agreement issues.

    - What firms should be doing to interest their staff in becoming partners and to develop them into partner candidates.

2. **Staff at CPA firms** who are interested in a career in public accounting and therefore want to know what they need to do to become partners. This includes the skills they need to master in order to qualify for partner and how the process of buying into equity ownership at a firm should work.

6

2

Why People Are Promoted to Partner

Why Firms Would Want to Make Someone a Partner

Before we get too far in this book, we must answer a basic question: Why would a CPA firm ever want to make someone a partner in the first place? Why would it want to share profits with more people?

The short answer is that it must be beneficial to both the firm and the new partner. A win-win, as the saying goes.

Here are nine reasons why firms are compelled to make someone a partner. Many are interrelated.

1. **New partners deserve the promotion to such a great extent that the firm can't afford NOT to award it.** These are managers who have consistently demonstrated their ability to significantly increase the firm's revenue growth, profitability and overall success, both currently and especially in the future. The firm needs to recognize these talents by admitting such managers to the ownership group, thus sharing profits and the firm's value with them. If the firm fails to recognize and reward partner candidates, they will eventually leave and find someplace else that appreciates their value. The firm's success and performance would be substantially hurt if the firm lost this person.

2. **Growth demands expansion of the partner ranks.** The firm's growth requires an increase in the number of partners it has. For example, a firm may decide that it wishes to maintain an average revenue per partner of $1.5M. Currently, the firm has eight partners and revenue of $12M. The firm may need to approach $13.5M before it feels justified in adding a ninth partner.

   However, the firm also reasons that there is a limit to the size of client base that a partner can manage while providing world-class service. So, many firms limit the size of each partner's client base. They need to bring in new partners to keep the base from growing too high.

3. **The firm must replace a retiring partner.** A partner with a healthy client base retires and the other partners are too busy to absorb the retiree's clients. The firm is fortunate to have a manager on board with the skills to manage the retiree's clients. Also, the manager may already have solid work experience with many of the retiree's clients. In cases such as these, partners often promote the manager to partner.

4. **A partner offer rewards a long-time manager with solid client service and technical skills.** The person is loyal and hard-working and has earned credibility with partners and staff. He or she may not have all the leadership and business development skills that the firm prefers its partners to have, but the partners nonetheless feel the person deserves the partner promotion. In many instances, the partners would have heart-burn if the person left due to being passed over for promotion. In these cases, the partner promotion has been earned and is a staff retention tactic.

5. **People are needed to write the partners' retirement checks.** 80% of all first-generation firms never make it to the second because of weak succession planning, including an insufficient number of younger partners to buy out the existing partners. By promoting a competent, loyal, skilled, hard-working manager to partner, the firm acquires one more person to share in the partner buyout burden.

6. **Partner promotions send a signal to the staff.** When the staff sees people promoted to partner periodically, it sends a message that if they work hard and smart to acquire partner-level skills

and experience, their efforts may eventually be recognized and rewarded with ownership. Caveat: Firms should never promote people who lack these partner-level skills to partner simply to send a message.

7. **It provides a spark to the partner group.** Some firms evolve over a long time without making any new partners. The result is an aging partner group that lacks energy and innovation and may be somewhat stagnant. Injecting deserving, skilled young people into the partner ranks may be just the shot in the arm the firm needs.

8. **The firm needs technical partners.** In an ideal world, a major criterion for promotion to partner is a track record of bringing in business. This is the most difficult trait for aspiring staff to acquire. Some firms find it a useful practice to periodically promote non-business-getting staff to partner because the firm needs technical partners to function at a very high level, supporting the other partners who are adept at business development. The person promoted must have demonstrated other valuable skills, such as client handling, loyalty, a strong work ethic and an ability to train staff.

   Firms usually find that there is a limit to the number of technical partners they can afford.

9. **It's part of a merger strategy.** When buyers merge in smaller firms with partners who are "younger" (i.e., not close to retirement) but possess skills similar to those of the buyer's existing partners and manage sizable client bases, the only way the seller's partners will agree to the merger is if they become partners in the buyer's firm.

Why Staff Should *Want* to Become Partners

Partners have it great. If a staff person really gets a proper, thorough understanding of why it's fantastic to become a partner in a CPA firm, there are almost no reasons for *not* wanting to be a partner. Well, there are a few, but we'll discuss them later in the chapter.

1. **The money.** Sorry, I probably shouldn't have led with this one. I struggled with where to put it. If I put it first, you may think I'm saying that money is everything, but I certainly don't feel that way. If I put it last, some might think it's the least important, but that is not the case either. If I bury it in the middle, it might not get your attention.

   In 2020, the income of equity partners in CPA firms under $20M in revenue (99% of all multipartner firms) averaged $300,000 to $500,000, depending on their size and location. This number is substantially higher for firms larger than $20M. This is more money than 95% or more of all people in North America earn and is almost always substantially higher than their parents earned. No question: the money is wonderful.

   As parents, we try to counsel our children on a career to pursue. Some parents advise their kids to pursue their passion, regardless of the hurdles. Others advise their children to pursue a noble career that will enable them to earn a nice living. I always have advised young people, including my own children, that it is quite possible to have both: a career that you are passionate about *and* that pays well. That's the overarching reason why staff should want to be a partner. If you are not passionate about the profession of public accounting, that may be a good reason not to pursue a partnership.

2. **Ownership,** from two points of view. First, as a partner, you will be an owner in a business (for 99% of you, it will be a *small* business) that is almost guaranteed to increase in value over time. For new partners, this increase may be three to ten times its original value. Second, as an owner of a small business, you will be an entrepreneur. As such, you will have virtually unlimited freedom and flexibility to run your part of the firm and decide how you spend your time.

3. **Challenging, interesting work.** The work performed by partners is much more sophisticated and challenging than staff-level work. The

focus of partner work shifts to solving people's problems, planning and relationships, as opposed to the more technical work of staff. Summary: Partner work is cool!

4. **Relationships with your clients.** It's been well-documented in numerous psychological studies that the happiest people are those who have healthy relationships with other people. Relationships improve the quality of their lives and bring them joy. When you are a partner, the major relationships in your life, besides your family and friends, are the clients you work with. Partners love their clients and clients love them back. Life doesn't get much better than that.

5. **Responsibility.** Virtually all partners manage a sizable client base. This could range from several hundred thousand dollars to several million dollars. Most partners find this high level of responsibility very satisfying. It's frustrating at times. Stressful at times. But it's enormously satisfying to be an owner in a CPA firm with the responsibility for acquiring, retaining and growing a client base.

6. **Prestige.** I've got to tread carefully on this one because it touches a little on ego and vanity. But who can blame someone for feeling great about the prestige that comes with becoming a partner in a highly reputable, successful CPA firm in one's community? Prestige will never be #1 on this list, but most newly promoted partners would admit (at least to themselves) how good the ego boost feels when they become a partner.

   Many partners have told me that it became easier to bring in business when they were able to tell people they were a partner in such and such a firm. It's the classic chicken or the egg argument. Were they more successful at business development because of their maturity and self-confidence, and the partner promotion was merely the icing on the cake? Or was the development of these traits possible only once the person was promoted to partner? This is one of those questions that have no answer.

7. **Staff to delegate to.** Certainly, people who are promoted to partner were delegating work to staff before their promotion. But when someone becomes a partner, the amount of work delegated to staff increases considerably. Evidence of this are these metrics from a recent Rosenberg MAP Survey: Managers average about 1,400 billable hours a year, while equity partners are around 1,100, lower

at bigger firms. That's a 300-hour gap, a 21% difference. It's kind of nice to have an army of people at your beck and call.

8. **Tenure.** This one is a bit tongue-in-cheek. Nowhere is it written in firms' partner agreements that partners can never be fired. But as a practical matter, unless someone commits egregious acts, there is very little chance of being terminated. CPA firms are very lax at holding partners accountable for their performance or behavior.

9. **Lack of accountability.** Pardon the sarcasm, but it would be an understatement to say that there is very little partner accountability at the vast majority of CPA firms. In #2 I wrote that partners have tremendous flexibility in how they work. Probably too much. If you are a manager asking yourself: "What's so good about being a partner?" does a low amount of accountability appeal to you?

Why Someone Might NOT Want to Be a Partner

There are two sides to every discussion. The previous section may have made it seem as if you'd have to be a fool *not* to want to be a partner. But being a partner isn't for everybody. The reasons listed below exclude issues not germane to this discussion, such as a desire to change careers, opportunities to join one's family business or boredom with accounting.

- **Long hours.** At most firms, when the staff leave, the partners are still working. Some feel it sends a negative message to the staff because it implies that there is an expectation for partners to work long hours and therefore make it difficult to enjoy a healthy work-life balance. Rosenberg MAP survey metrics corroborate this: Partners average around 2,410 total work hours but the staff average is 2,280, a difference of 130 overtime hours.

  Counter to this: I defy anyone to find a highly successful executive in any organization, regardless of the compensation, who doesn't put in extra time. If your goal is to be a 9-to-5er, then you shouldn't be a CPA firm partner.

- **Liability exposure.** When you are an owner of a business, you are liable for legal issues. For CPA firms, this is mainly malpractice.

Counter to this: As a practical matter, in my 20 years of experience, I've seen an extremely small percentage of firms have significant legal problems. When they do, it's rarely catastrophic.

- **Partner buyouts.** Almost all CPA firms have a substantial unrecorded liability for future partner buyouts. Younger partners often have concern about the affordability of those payments, especially if there is legitimate concern about the firm staying in business when key partners retire.

Counter to this: The vast majority of CPA firms have partner buyout plans that work very successfully, without putting undue financial stress on the partners. In fact, buying out older partners will most likely be the best investment a partner ever makes.

Another counter: If the buyout plan looks unaffordable, the partners can always pursue an upward merger to resolve this problem.

- **Stress.** No question. When you are a hard-driving senior officer of a dynamic, profitable company, there is stress. Meeting deadlines. Handling clients' unreasonable demands. Hiring and training staff that turn over at a high rate. For an owner, stress is undeniable.

Counter to this: Can you show me anyone who is a highly successful professional, especially a business owner, who is free of stress? Here's a lesson in psychology, taught to me by my psychologist wife, Dr. Ellen Rosenberg. There are two kinds of stress: Good stress and bad stress. Good stress, though it doesn't always feel good, drives you to achieve better things, makes you creative and stronger. Bad stress is not good for your health. Examples are a tragic death of a family member or a natural disaster. Most of the stresses of being a partner in a CPA firm are good stresses.

- **It takes a long time to make partner.** *Accounting Today* reported that it takes 10 or more years to make partner at two-thirds of all firms. My anecdotal experience is that most new partners are 32 to 40 years of age. That means they will work 11 to 18 years before making partner.

Counter to this: There is none, other than the old saying that patience is a virtue. I personally think firms take too long to promote staff to partner, so I see why some staff are unwilling to wait.

So staff, if you like your firm, you like your work and you want to have a successful, lucrative professional career, these obstacles should not stop you from pursuing a partnership.

Why YOU Might Not Want Someone to Be a Partner

Many firms make the mistake of admitting to the partnership someone who will not be a strong contributing member of the group. They miss the signs that this person will be a bad fit.

The following red flags may signal a potential future challenge in the partnership. Consider whether your candidate

1. **Lacks skills your firm *needs today* to be successful.** If you are in dire need of a rainmaker, you probably don't have room for another partner who has no skills or interest in bringing in business. This can be problematic without a separate solution (e.g. hiring someone for business development). Same goes for technical, client service and team development skill sets.

2. **Has difficulty meeting expectations, makes promises and doesn't deliver.** Most firm members have good intentions, but when it comes to partner-candidates, individuals need to meet their commitments reliably.

3. **Is difficult to work with.** While not everyone needs to be a star mentor that staff are clamoring to learn from, admitting a new partner that no one wants to work with will damage your firm's ability to retain employees and run an efficient practice.

4. **Has financial troubles, substance abuse or similar undesirable traits.** Just like in marriage, don't plan on fixing somebody once you're in the relationship.

5. **Doesn't support group decisions or firm policies.** They might say yes in the meeting (or not), but then turn their backs and tell staff how they think an initiative is a bad idea. They don't uphold the partnership's position. A classic example: resisting technology changes and sticking with the old way, including requiring less experienced team members to comply.

14

How do you screen out these potential partners, especially if they've been hearing that after a certain number of years they'll likely be able to make partner?

Start by getting very clear as an existing partner group on what your expectations are of the role of a partner. Is it OK for a partner not to mentor? Not to bring in new business? Not to take on leadership initiatives at the firm? Any of these, maybe even all, could be fine at your firm (if, say, you're in need of a strong QC partner). But if it's not, don't let someone in who can't step up to the plate. You'll hold it against them, creating an unhealthy and unproductive dynamic.

Partners: Sell Your Staff on What a Great Job You Have!

Talk to your young staff about why being a CPA firm partner is an awesome career. But don't stop there. Describe the benefits of being a staff person at *your* firm: the interesting, challenging work they'll be assigned, the excellent compensation potential and advancement opportunities, their own personal baptism to the world of business. Then watch what happens.

A star will be born.

Give your stars access to cutting-edge technology. Provide constant training and feedback and flexible work options, especially for people who want to combine careers with raising a family. Build team spirit and go beyond it to a team orientation to servicing clients. Make your staff understand how their work contributes to the overall success of the firm, and more than that, why they should *care*.

3

What Is a Partner?

We've all heard the names given various generations of people over the past century. The Lost Generation. The Greatest (WWII) Generation. The Silent Generation. Baby Boomers. Gen X. Millennials. Gen Z. Though I don't know of any studies on this, I'm quite sure that every generation of CPA firm ownership has complained—bitterly—about the younger generation.

Baby Boomers and Gen Xers love to complain that today's staff don't want to be partners. They cite this as a major reason why it's so difficult to bring in new partners.

It's my opinion that the problem is not so much that young people don't *want* to be partners. They simply don't know what it *means* to be a partner and they don't know what it *takes* to become a partner.

This chapter explains
- Skills and experience needed to make partner.
- What a partner is ... and is not.
- What a partner does.
- Why it's so great to be a partner ... if partners would only take the time to explain it to the staff.

Bringing in New Partners:
Thresholds and Core Competencies

There are quite a few items on the list that appears in a few pages. Before listing them all, I want to focus briefly on four really important items:

1. **Trust.** This doesn't mean trust that the new partners won't cheat on their expense reports or steal money. It's trust that they will always be honest and truthful and make sound judgments in the performance of their work and their conduct within and outside the firm and will never jeopardize the firm's reputation and commitment to quality. Trust that they will always do the right thing. A firm should never make someone a partner unless it totally trusts the person.

2. **The beer/wine test.** I apologize for this colloquial expression, but it captures the point. A potential partner may possess most or all of the skills needed to be a partner: technical, ability to manage relationships, work ethic, bringing in business. But one additional attribute is crucial: Are you proud to call the new partner a "partner"? Do you feel good about introducing your new partner to clients and others? Do you respect the new partner? Will you enjoy that person's company? This doesn't mean that partners need to be best friends or even see each other socially. It simply means that from time to time, you'd enjoy having a stein of beer or a glass of wine with your new partner because you enjoy their company.

3. **Business development.** This is easily the most controversial criterion in the CPA profession for becoming an equity partner. Some firms believe that a staffer must prove his or her skill as a business-getter to qualify for partner because they firmly believe that's what partners *do*: drive the firm by bringing in business. These firms would never consider promoting someone to equity partner unless he or she has brought in a targeted amount of business.

   Other firms do not have *strict* requirements for bringing business to become an equity partner. These firms would certainly prefer that new partners be business-getters. But for the following reasons, firms often promote non-business-getters to partners:

   - The partners are not great business-getters *themselves*, so they are reluctant to hold new partners to a standard they themselves can't meet. As evidence, this anecdotal experience is shared by many of my fellow consultants: At firms under $10M, perhaps only 20% of the partners would be considered truly effective business-getters. Not rainmakers, but simply proficient at bringing in business.

- The firm feels it has enough partners who are business-getters and what it really needs are a few partners whose primary focus is technical. The firm feels a strong need to bolster the work quality area of the firm, even if it means bringing in non-business-getters as partners.

- Some firms are fortunate to enjoy such an enviable rate of revenue growth that they periodically need to add new equity partners to manage their ever-expanding client base. A related situation is where a partner retires and the remaining partners are all too busy to absorb the retiring partner's clients. In these cases, firms often bring in new partners to manage clients, even if they are not business-getters.

- There is a tradition among firms under, say, $15M to reward competent long-time managers by making them partner. These managers are great, highly valued employees but lack business development and leadership skills. Promotion to partner is first, a reward for their hard work and proficiency. Second, the partners reason that if they don't promote a loyal, valuable staff person to partner, the person will eventually quit, and they can't afford to lose that person.

Generally speaking, the larger the firm, the more likely that bringing in business is a solid criterion for promotion to equity partner. There isn't a right or wrong position on this. It's up to each individual firm to set partner criteria for business development that they are comfortable with.

4. **Client management experience.** This goes beyond the technical performance of the work. It's responsibility for managing client relationships and satisfying their needs. It includes engagement planning, billing, growing the firm's services with clients and getting referrals from them.

No firm's criteria for promotion to partner include all of the items in the list that follows. It is a compilation of policies and documents I have seen while working with many great firms. I encourage you to review this list, modify it and add to it until the end result is a policy your partners are comfortable with.

All of the items here are important. Those that your humble author considers the most important are in boldface type.

Bringing in a New Partner: Thresholds and Core Competencies

Intangibles

1. **Inspires TRUST. Integrity, honesty, sound ethical behavior and judgment**
2. **Has credibility with partners and staff**
3. **Encourages client confidence: Clients are comfortable calling the partner-potential first rather than the originating partner.**
4. has strong work ethic
5. Shows loyalty and commitment
6. **Is a team player**
7. **Can pass the "beer/wine" test**
8. has communication and interpersonal skills
9. Has leadership skills and high self-esteem

Financial and legal

1. **Is willing and able to buy in**
2. **Is willing to take on retirement obligations**
3. **Is willing to sign a nonsolicitation agreement**
4. Demonstrates personal financial stability

Business development

1. **Originates X amount of business**
2. Constantly pursues meetings with clients, prospects and referral sources to get new business
3. Actively seeks opportunities to cross-sell additional services to existing clients

4. Has been active for at least several years in building up a network of business contacts
5. Has distinguished self as an expert in at least one service or industry

Production and client management

1. **Manages X number of clients (billing, relationship and engagement management)**
2. **Achieves X billable hours ...**
3. **... at X realization**

Technical

1. Demonstrates a high level of analytical and problem-solving skills; solves clients' problems
2. **Exhibits enough technical skill so the firm is comfortable that once the partner candidate has finished a client project, no one else needs to review it to make sure it was done right Candidate has proven ability to complete highly technical projects with minimal assistance.**

Supervision

1. **Has solid experience and effectiveness in supervising staff**
2. Is a delegator
3. Is able to develop others

Administration

1. Follows and complies with all firm policies, procedures and deadlines
2. Is willing and able to perform administrative duties as required by your firm

Basic Role and Expectations of Partners

The following apocryphal vignette plays out at partner retreats on a regular basis: The partners brainstorm what is expected of partners at their firm. They have a spirited, productive discussion that results in a dozen items written on a flipchart. All of a sudden, one of the partners yells, "Oh, no!" The startled partners ask him what's wrong. He points at the flipchart: "None of us qualify!"

As with the previous list, there is not one firm whose policy on what a partner is reads exactly like the one below. This is a collection of what I have seen at many great firms I have had the pleasure of working with.

Here are 17 basic expectations of partners. Think twice before promoting anyone who can't meet them all.

1. **Drive** firm growth, profitability and success.

2. **Be trustworthy**. It's not about stealing money. Instead, it's about exercising good judgment, never circumventing policies and procedures and upholding professional standards and ethics.

3. **Be a leader**. Partners earn credibility with fellow partners and the staff by being good role models, inspiring others to follow their lead. The firm is evaluated by *the partners'* conduct.

4. **Manage** the firm, to the extent that the partner has a formal role in this area. This includes the MP, Executive Committee member, Compensation Committee member, or a PIC (partner in charge) of an office, department or industry team.

5. **Manage client relationships and engagements** effectively. Be attentive to their needs; establish strong client loyalty to maximize retention. Move clients upscale and grow their fees, while giving them the full value of your attention. Bill and collect promptly.

6. **Train and mentor staff.** Don't just be a "nice" partner; also help staff develop, grow and advance under your tutelage. This will impact staff retention. Treat staff with *at least* as much respect as clients.

7. **Bring in business.** Contribute to business development in *some* way; develop and cultivate referral sources.

8. **Provide outstanding client service**. Exceed clients' expectations. Deliver on commitments.

9. **Be a team player**; develop a strong team beneath you; ensure that your largest clients have multiple touch points within the firm; share work with others. Always be willing to assist other partners and staff as needed.

10. **Achieve your written goals**, both production and intangible. Fulfill your role in the firm.

11. **Push work down** to staff wherever possible; do only partner-level work. Keep the staff busy.

12. Live and breathe the firm's **core values**, every day. Respect the firm, its decisions and its partners.

13. **Protect the firm.** Establish required technical skills, then keep them updated and maintained; never do work beyond your capability. Never stop learning. Commit to the highest professional **ethics.**

14. Be a **good corporate citizen**. Obey the firm's policies and procedures, even if you don't agree with them. Treat people respectfully. Respond in a timely manner to voicemails, emails, etc.

15. Practice good **communications** at all levels. Let people know what's going on with you.

16. Be **accountable** for your performance and behavior.

17. Do all of the above as a **full-time partner**. Partners give it their all. They don't have other commitments, such as managing a separate business or fulfilling a role outside the firm, perhaps in a charitable or civic organization, that prevent them from performing their partner duties on a 24/7 basis.

The Realities of Being a Partner

You're an owner. As such, you get paid based on the firm's earnings, not as an employee.

You pay for your ownership. New owners in any business must pay money to acquire their ownership. At CPA firms, this is called a new partner buy-in. Since CPA firms have a substantial street value, it's reasonable that new partners should be required to purchase their interest in the firm.

As a partner, you get a vote. Big deal! Most firms don't take formal votes. Instead, they discuss an issue, determine a consensus and act on the decision. If partners really want their "votes" to count, it's up to each of them to articulate their position on issues at hand and try to influence other partners to see things their way. So a vote is really more of a right to attend partner meetings and influence decisions.

Who owns clients and staff? Hint: It's not individual partners. It's the *firm*. This means that a partner who decides to leave the firm and join another cannot take clients and staff. Of course, there is no law that says clients and staff cannot join the departed partner. But there *is* an enforceable partner agreement (80-90% of all firms have such an agreement) that prevents departed partners from taking clients and staff and requires them to pay liquidated damages to the firm.

Partner buyout obligation. By accepting a firm's offer to become an equity partner, a new partner becomes obligated to join with other partners, both present and future, to buy out the interest of departed partners. The flip side of this is that new partners will get a buyout when *they* retire.

What Partners Are and Are NOT Entitled To

Partners ARE entitled to

1. Attend partner meetings and retreats.
2. Have their capital returned upon leaving the firm.
3. Make decisions on client engagements.
4. Receive regular communications from management regarding what is going on in the firm.
5. Vote on matters specified in the firm's partner agreement.
6. Be paid based on performance.
7. Have their interest in the firm bought out as stipulated in the partner agreement.

Partners are NOT entitled to

1. Pull rank.
2. Be given a lifetime waiver on performance feedback.
3. Do whatever they want to do, *whenever* they want to.
4. Participate in managing the firm. That's management's job.
5. Get paid a lot of money without *earning* it.
6. Do lower-level staff or admin work and be paid partner-level compensation for it.
7. Do what's best for themselves to the detriment of the firm.
8. Be Lone Rangers (act alone; nobody knows where they are).
9. Abuse staff or behave disrespectfully toward them.
10. Take clients if they leave the firm to practice elsewhere.
11. Retain clients if they fail to service them properly.
12. Be unaccountable for their performance and behavior.

Partner
(Equity or Non-Equity)
Job Description

General

- A partner is first and foremost a leader in the firm. Partners always set an example for others to follow because the firm is evaluated by its partners' conduct.

- Partners have three primary duties: Bring in business, completely satisfy clients' needs and help staff learn and grow.

- Partners are "impact players" who make clear and measurable contributions to the firm's growth and profitability.

- Technical skills are a given. They are the ante to get into the game.

- Partners make decisions that are aligned with the firm's strategic plan and vision.

Specific duties

1. Bring in business. Contribute to business development and marketing in *some* way; develop and cultivate referral sources. Include other firm members on sales calls. Understand that, when it comes to business development, you can't not try.

2. Train and mentor staff so they can advance.

3. Be constantly alert to opportunities to hire talent.

4. Manage client relationships and engagements effectively; be attentive to their needs; establish strong client loyalty to maximize retention. Take clients upscale.

5. Serve as clients' primary business advisor.

6. Establish other firm members as key touch points with larger clients so that if the partner suddenly leaves the firm, the clients will stay.

7. Develop and lead strong teams.

8. Become the firm's go-to person for *something*.

9. Be a good corporate citizen. Obey policies and procedures, even if the partner disagrees with them. Treat people respectfully. Respond timely to voice mails, emails, etc.

10. Live and breathe the firm's core values, *every day*.

11. Push down work to the staff wherever possible; do only partner-level work. Understand that a partner should be working ON the business, not IN it.

12. Keep the staff busy. Never lose sight of this critical partner duty; never assume other partners are handling this.

13. Bill and collect promptly and aggressively.

14. Ensure that client engagement letters and all other required agreements and correspondence with clients are executed for each engagement.

15. Take on minimal, and preferably no, admin duties (i.e., duties that can be delegated to admin staff).

16. Be fiscally responsible 24/7; never be off duty.

How New Partner Duties Change from Manager Duties

This is one of the grayest areas in bringing in new partners. It has perplexed CPA firms for decades.

Here is the typical scenario. The firm has had one or more managers on board for 10 to 20 years. They have made their mark primarily with their technical skills, doing great work with clients, showing tremendous loyalty and work ethic. They generally lack business development and to a lesser extent, leadership skills, but they have become indispensable to the partners, who rely on them heavily to service their clients. The partners would have heartburn if these managers left the firm.

Now, one or more of these managers are promoted to partner.

- How does their job change? How *should* it change?

- They may not have been expected to bring in business because of their partners' heavy reliance on them to service their clients. Should the firm now expect these new partners to bring in business? To what extent are they expected to build their own client base?

- Do they continue working on the same clients they did as managers?

To shed light on this practice, we polled 20 managing partners of local multipartner CPA firms from across the country. Almost all of the firms' annual revenue was $5-$25M.

Summary of Responses. As is always the case when issues of general practice are discussed, there was a wide variety in the 20 responses we received. Here is the consensus of the responses:

1. When managers are promoted to partner, the role doesn't change very much, especially in the beginning years. New partners almost always continue to work on the same clients they were responsible for prior to the promotion.

2. The major change is that now they are expected to delegate work to managers so they can function as partners. This new partner role includes not only delegating the work but developing the managers' leadership skills. This frees up the new partners to (a) take on additional clients other partners transfer to them and, most importantly, (b) do business development.

3. For decades, CPA firms have debated the pros and cons of requiring people to bring in business to become eligible for partnership. Our 20 firms reflect this diversity of opinion. Several firms feel it is important to have a balance between business-getting and technical partners. However, more than half of the firms feel that new partners *should* develop business.

4. Several of the firms that were more insistent on BD as a requirement for becoming a partner stated that people with partner aspirations should have been engaged in BD activities well before being considered for partner.

5. An important factor in all these issues is the increasing incidence of firms having two kinds of partners: non-equity and equity. Many firms may not be so insistent on requiring business-getting skills to become a non-equity partner, but bringing in business is very likely to be a criterion for advancement to equity partner.

6. Several firms stated that they like their new partners to have distinguished themselves as experts in a niche or specialty service.

4

The Path to Partner

The old-school way of developing staff into partners was very simple:

- Staff are bountiful. Those with the right stuff move up; we'll move the others out and hire a new crop to replace them.

- It's up to the staff to pull themselves up by their own bootstraps and make their mark. Nobody showed *us* how to make partner. Nobody held *our* hands.

- It's up to the staff to tell *us* that they want to be partners. Unless and until they show us this ambition, we won't talk to them about becoming a partner.

- Bringing in business can't be taught. You're either born with it or you're not.

- And while we are on the subject of business development, we all know from experience that marketing must be done nights and weekends. Clients are too busy during the day. And we need the days to get our billable hours in. So a partner must commit to working long hours, including nights and weekends, and be willing to sacrifice his or her personal life for the firm.

Not much of a clear or easy path in those days, was there?

Thankfully, this major area of CPA firm management has improved dramatically over the years. As with all changes, there will always be firms that lag behind and stubbornly stick with old practices. But truly progressive firms get it and are proactive about developing a path to partnership for their staff.

Skills Staff Need to Make Partner: In General

This list started with numerous discussions I had with CPA firm managing partners. I supplemented it with written surveys. The question I asked: "What does it take to be successful at a CPA firm?"

1. Sharpen your **interpersonal and communication skills**, with both clients and firm personnel:
    - Speak clearly; learn how to get your point across succinctly, with focus and without fumbling.
    - Write articulate, coherent, concise emails.
    - Gain the clients' confidence. Work as much as possible in the field. That's where you learn.
    - Learn the client's business, not just their accounting systems.
    - When clients are comfortable with you, they'll call *you* instead of your supervisor.

2. **Be a self-starter**; develop a reputation for reliability; **someone who gets things done:**
    - Take responsibility for the job from beginning to end. **Own your projects.**
    - Before going to the supervisor for help, try to solve the problem yourself—but don't spend excessive time on it.
    - **NEVER, EVER submit work for review if you *know* it needs further work or is wrong.**

3. Demonstrate that you are passionate about your job and your work. **Show enthusiasm.**

4. **Ask lots of questions** but show that you have given thought to them first. Figure out what you can before taking up time.

5. **Know what you don't know.** Avoid amassing hours and hours on a project when you don't really understand what you're doing.

6. **Make budgets and deadlines your friends.** Always know what the time budgets and deadlines are for your assignments. Ask if you're not told.

7. **Ask what the firm expects of you in terms of annual billable hours and realization.**

8. **Be proactive in finding work** with supervisors when you have unassigned blocks in your calendar. If on Thursday or Friday, you know you have little work for the following week, don't wait until Monday morning to ask around for work.

9. **Ask for performance feedback after *every* job;** don't wait until the supervisor gets around to it. Don't try to "escape" without getting the feedback or asking for feedback.

10. **It's OK to strive for work-life balance, but understand that meeting *clients'* needs comes *first*.**

11. **Be proficient with technology.**

12. **Learn all the services your firm provides** so you can spot additional opportunities for helping clients.

13. **Be self-confident.** Don't hide from partners and managers. Gain their confidence. **Partners and managers like to see young staff be assertive and comfortable making conversation with older adults.**

14. Oh, yes ... master the **technical requirements** of your job. (This is really a given.)

Now let's build on these skills to transform this list into skills needed to make partner. Add the following:

15. **Develop deep client relationships** so that over time, the clients want to talk with *you*, not the partner.

16. **Be assigned a list of smaller clients** that you are responsible for. Not just the work, but engagement management (planning, billing, collection, work review, etc.), client relationships and cross-selling.

17. **Learn to become a great staff mentor**, one who is skilled at helping younger staff learn and grow. Partner candidates should be the kind of people that staff want to work with.

18. **Continuously develop and refine business development skills** and translate them into business origination.

19. **Be productive.** Achieve targeted levels of billable hour productivity at high levels of realization.

20. **Continue to build technical skills** so that you reach the point where (a) you can do the work correctly, with minimal corrections needed by the reviewer and (b) you can perform highly complex projects, normally handled at the partner level, because the partners have confidence in you.

Skills Staff Need to Make Partner: Business Development

Our book *CPA Firm Growth: Keys to Practice Development*, https://rosenbergassoc.com/product/cpa-firm-growth-keys-to-practice-development/, is 217 pages of A to Z material on what CPA firms and accounting firm personnel need to do to achieve revenue growth. Here is our attempt to distill that tome into a few pages.

These business development skills are the skills and activities that firms want to see staff display continuously to consider them partner candidates. As stated earlier, CPA firm partners' business development skills range dramatically, from the rainmaker to those who wouldn't see a sales opportunity if it hit them in the nose. The extent to which these skills are required to become a partner is, of course, entirely up to each firm.

1. The best source of new business and increased revenue is the firm's *current* clients. Partner-potentials need to thoroughly understand all firm services and continuously evaluate which of their clients could benefit from additional services. Partner candidates should meet frequently with clients to *ask* for the business.

   Here is a critical mindset that every member of the firm should have: Identifying additional services to provide clients, often called cross-selling, is a way that CPAs are *proactive* in helping clients. They do this because they know from experiences with other clients that these additional services will make companies more profitable and successful. Cross-selling should never be confused with selling services to clients that they don't want or need, an activity that is unethical.

2. The best source of new business and increased revenue is with the firm's *current* clients, Part II. It would be great if *they* came to *you* for the expanded services, and you would be ecstatic if *they* made unsolicited referrals to you. Some do. Most do not. They need to be asked. If you don't ask, you don't get.

3. Network. This includes being active in the community and developing the fine art of small talk so you can work the room at networking events. Partner candidates should participate regularly in networking activities, not only for business development purposes, but for polishing their skills as networkers.

4. Business development requires planning. Don't expect to call a client or prospect *today* to set up a time to meet with them *today*. If you *always* eat lunch alone or with co-workers, you aren't trying hard enough to bring in business. A review of a partner candidate's calendar should show a regular stream of meetings scheduled in advance with busy clients and prospects.

5. Partner potentials must understand that BD is a contact sport. The more times at bat, the more hits. Having two prospect meetings a month and landing one is a .500 batting average, great in baseball but a prescription for failure in BD. It's much better to have ten prospect meetings a month and land three of them. Bad news is a lower batting average of .300. Good news is getting three new clients instead of one.

6. In BD activities, specialization beats the scattergun approach to selling every time. Specialization makes selling easier because clients and prospects prefer buying from experts. With special-ization, prospects often call *you* instead of the other way around. And when you sell a service in which you have specialized expertise, you can charge a premium price and the client will gladly pay it. Have you developed specialized expertise in oner or more fields, if so do you use it in your BD activities?

7. Differentiate yourself. When you introduce yourself to a prospect, develop a style and approach that shows how you are different from and more special than other CPA firms.

8. Seek training in BD. Selling is not a genetic trait. It's a skill that *can* be learned. Training *does* work. But like most forms of training, it won't be effective unless (a) the training is done continuously, as opposed to a one-shot-deal, and (b) the knowledge learned is practiced on real clients and prospects. Partner candidates should demonstrate this commitment to BD training.

9. Learn from the pros. Partner candidates should be accompanying partners on their meetings with prospects.

10. A goal that is not in writing is merely a wish. Be formal about it. Create written goals for your BD activities. As much as possible, these goals should include the number of BD meetings you will convene and specific names of prospects.

11. Be active in complementary marketing activities such as giving speeches, writing articles and blog posts, participating in seminars and keeping up on social media. Focus on the ones that are most appealing to you.

I recently heard the MP of $50M Hogan Taylor talk about what his firm does to develop staff as business-getters. Randy Nail took over the reins of HT in 2009 shortly after the merger of two equal $10M firms and has presided over the firm's phenomenal growth. This is what HT does:

- Partners and staff work in teams.

- Partners take staff on sales calls. Nail feels too much business development is often done alone.

- Staff are trained in having conversations.

- Staff are sent to multiyear external leadership development organizations.

- The Hogan Taylor university stresses soft skills from Day 1.

- The company holds lots of lunch and learns.

Skills Staff Need to Make Partner: Being a Good Boss

The CPA profession has made considerable progress over the decades in the way partners treat staff. In the dark days, CPA firms treated staff as if they were a dime a dozen, disrespectfully, with a sweatshop mentality. The philosophy was up or out. The word "mentor" was not in the CPA's dictionary.

But for years now, many CPA firms have adopted the credo that "Our staff are just as important as our clients." Firms need to do a lot more work on walking this talk, but it's heartening that they at least *aspire* to this dual focus.

I have read many articles and studies on what's most important to employees. The most compelling finding: The #1 reason why employees—anyone in any business, not just CPA firm staff—leave their company is a poor relationship with their boss. At CPA firms, the bosses are the collective group of people, mostly the partners and managers, who supervise staff.

A good boss is both of the following:

- **A nice person.** Upbeat. Caring. Respectful. Approachable. Polite. Courteous. Professional. Fun to be with. But while it's fantastic for bosses to be nice, it's not enough. Not even close.

- **Someone who helps staff learn and grow.** A good boss increases the staff's knowledge, experience and skills, stretching their abilities while inspiring them. Says Al Kutchins, MP of Chicago-based KRD: "It is the responsibility of young partners to bring up the next generation of partners behind them."

People who firms consider for promotion to partner should consistently exhibit the following to be good bosses:

1. Engage staff.
2. Challenge staff and stretch their abilities.
3. Counsel and mentor.
4. Show an interest in staff beyond their jobs.
5. Proactively help staff qualify for promotions.

6. Inspire confidence in the staff; show trust.

7. Let the staff make mistakes.

8. Treat staff like equals, not subordinates. Never pull rank.

9. Treat staff respectfully.

10. Be respectful of the staff's time and other commitments.

11. Be a good listener.

12. Provide great one-on-one training. Show patience.

13. Set a good example in work habits.

14. Avoid the "my way or the highway" attitude.

Measuring Staff Performance on the Path to Partner

There are many ways to measure the performance of staff on the path to making partner. As is my style, I will present far more measures than most firms actually use. But I doubt you'll perceive any of the methods here as unimportant. They are not listed in any particular order of importance.

Stellar performance appraisals. This includes oral feedback that is shared among the partners.

Masterful management of client responsibility. Before staff are considered for partner, they should have been assigned a small client base to manage. This includes performing the work, managing client relationships and attending to all the administrative aspects of engagement management, such as billing, collection and planning. Mastery is evidenced by the following:

- Clients call the potential partner instead of the prior or originating partner. Some clients prefer this.

- Clients are retained.

- The partner potential has moved the firm's services to clients upscale.

- Realization targets are achieved. Write-offs are at an acceptable level.

- Projects are delivered on time. Billings and collections are timely.
- Potential partners achieve formal, written goals. All managers should participate in a goal-setting program, just like partners.

Skillful management of staff.

- Staff give the manager strong scores on upward evaluations.
- The manager is effective in mentoring staff and giving them timely performance evaluations, as evidenced when staff advance under the partner potential's tutelage.
- The manager exhibits strong supervisory skills, including delegation, training, review of work, timely job-by-job evaluation and accessibility.

Business development. Potential partners are both active in BD activities and successful in originating business. They demonstrate a healthy, positive attitude toward bringing in business.

Technical skills.

- The partner potential manages multiple projects at the same time.
- When the partner potential's work is reviewed, minimal changes are required.
- The manager works on highly complex matters so that partners delegate these projects confidently.

Productivity. Achieves the firm's targeted billable hours at strong levels of realization consistently for many years. Productivity also relates to nonbillable activities such as staff management, billing, collection and performance of assigned firm-wide projects.

Specialization. Over time, the partner potential has acquired one or more specialized skills and/or industry expertise and is considered a go-to person in these areas by the firm.

The baseball umpire's credo: The partner potential is mobile, assertive and loud. He or she speaks up at partner meetings and is influential, assertive and self-confident. The person seeks responsibility.

Strong work ethic. The partner potential is willing and able to work extra hours to get the job done, ensuring that clients' needs and deadlines are met.

How Firms Create a Path to Partner

"I think nothing is more important than what a firm does to create partners. I mean from Day 1 of someone's career. Or maybe when a person is identified as a star. It's critical what the firm does to nurture that person so that they become a partner someday."

Harry Steindler, Partner
MichaelSilver (Chicago)

Here is what the best firms do to create a path to partnership. These practices are not ranked strictly, but items at the top of the list are more common and effective than those toward the bottom. However, all the items are important.

1. **Firms maintain a formal mentoring program.** Keys to effective mentoring programs:

   - There needs to be a firm-wide mentoring champion.

   - Limit mentors to those who have the skills for it.

   - Mentees can choose mentors, but be careful not to overload one mentor with too many protégés.

   - Mentors advise staff where they stand in the firm and what they need to do to advance.

   - Mentoring meetings should occur at least monthly.

   - Mentors should make mentees feel safe.

   - Mentors help mentees set goals.

   - Mentors are usually not the best people to conduct performance evaluations.

   - Mentors should not be assigned permanently.

2. **Firms send staff to outside leadership development programs.** The better programs convene multiple sessions over a period of time ranging from several months to two or three years.

3. **A huge part of a partner's job is to develop people.** Firms must reward what they expect. Partners' compensation should include a meaningful factor for the extent that staff advanced under their tutelage. Partners should make clear, impactful contributions to developing and retaining staff.

4. **Staff attend high-level client meetings to observe partners' conduct and style, even if their time is not billable.** As much as possible, staff should prepare the agenda and prepare minutes of the meetings.

5. **Partners rarely go on sales calls alone.** They take staff with them.

6. **Early on, identify staff who have star potential.** Says Jennifer Wilson of ConvergenceCoaching: "Star performers are valuable because they rise above others in initiative, intention and investment. They are driven to seek the next level in their careers. Communicate this to the staff and see how interested they are in being on a partner track."

7. **Partners proactively help staff become partners.** The stars are given plum assignments and opportunities to work with the firm's best clients. The firm errs on the side of giving the stars challenging work projects at an early stage in their development. Stars get higher salary increases and bonuses than the other staff.

   Some firms are concerned that giving certain staff star treatment will alienate average or marginal staff. Get over it. Giving special attention to your above-average staff is far more important than appeasing the ordinary or marginal people. Besides, if you compensate the stars the same as the others, it will upset the stars. You can't win!

   Treat your stars like partners before they actually become partners. Let them lead. Keep them engaged. Err on the side of promoting them too soon.

8. **Adopt the Gradual Release of Responsibility Model** of training (from Jennifer Wilson of ConvergenceCoaching). This is particularly

effective when a partner or manager is teaching a staffer a complex project. It consists of four steps, in this order:

- I do/ you watch.
- I do/you help.
- You do/I help.
- You do/I watch.

9. **Provide long-term training in business development.**

10. **Give staff responsibility for managing clients.** As the staff earn promotions to senior and manager, begin to assign small clients to them to give them the experience of managing engagements and client relationships.

11. **Involve them in a formal, written goal-setting program.**

12. **Encourage staff to pursue niches and specialties.**

13. **Partner potentials should be educated in the business of public accounting.** They should understand how the firm makes money and what holds profitability back. They should understand how CPA firms are managed and what makes them successful and efficient.

14. **Assign partner candidates to firm initiatives in service and technical areas.**

15. **Managers and non-equity partners should attend portions of equity partner meetings and partner retreats.**

16. **Managers should undergo the same performance appraisal process as partners, with the same criteria for evaluation.**

12 Questions to Ask of Staff

From Jennifer Wilson of ConvergenceCoaching.

1. What do you envision for your career in one year? In three years?

2. What do you view as your strengths and gifts?

3. What do you most like to do in your position right now?

4. What would you most like to try doing?

5. What do you like least in your position right now? Why? What would you like to see changed in your role as a result of this?

6. What skills do you want to develop to further succeed at the firm?

7. What other skills are you interested in acquiring?

8. What more can I, as your coach or mentor, or the firm do to improve your job satisfaction and assist you in being more successful?

9. What other areas of the firm are you interested in learning about?

10. What questions do you have about your career and its progression?

11. What should I know about you personally? What do you want to know about me?

12. What else would you like to discuss?

What It Takes to Advance

CPA firms have many different titles or positions. We will address the most common:

- Staff
- Senior
- Manager

Throughout this book I often use the term "staff" to refer to anyone who is not at the partner level. This is different from a "staff level" associate, who typically has only a few years or less of experience in public accounting.

This section addresses what it takes to advance from staff to senior and from senior to manager. The next section will address what it takes to advance to partner.

What It Takes to Advance

Title	Position Description	Next Promotion	What It Takes to Advance
Staff	• Is entry level • Works on one job at a time • Does not supervise staff • Mainly focuses on learning basic technical skills • Rarely reports to a partner	**Senior**	• Has the ability to senior small jobs • Hits annual charge hour budget with acceptable realization • Has mastered basic technical work • Doesn't repeat mistakes • Has 2-3 years as a staff person
Senior	• Runs jobs in the field • Mostly does one job at a time, but not always • Supervises staff • Has heavy client contact • Has lots of partner contact	**Manager**	• Jobs delivered to manager or partner need minimal change • Is a skillful supervisor • Is productive; realizable • Has partner or permanent manager potential • Has credibility with staff and partners • Has 2-3 years as a senior

How Long Should It Take to Make Partner?

This is a post from our Rosenberg blog.

Not too long ago, *Accounting Today* published a very interesting piece of research titled "The Long Path to Partner." The polling question: How many years does it take to make partner at your firm?

The results:

- Less than 5 years   9%
- 5-7 years   12%
- 8-9 years   12%
- 10-13 years   30%
- More than 13 years   17%
- Don't know   20%

I'll wager that the "don't know" firms are mostly in the 10 years or more categories, with the majority more than 13. So I extrapolate that at roughly two-thirds of all firms, it takes 10 or more years to make partner, which translates to an age range in the mid-30s. **Why does it take so long?**

The quick, expected response. I have asked this question of CPA firm partners on numerous occasions. Most of them say the long period of apprenticeship is necessary because it takes that long to acquire all of the necessary technical, supervisory, leadership, interpersonal and business-getting skills and to gain credibility with clients.

Contrast this to the medical and legal professions. Doctors are ready to practice their life-saving skills in their late 20s and early 30s. Lawyers often make partner in their early 30s. It's hard to imagine that the skills needed to be a CPA firm partner are more technically demanding than those of a partner in a medical or legal practice.

A "business" reason? At many firms, the promotion to equity partner often depends on whether or not the firm can afford to or needs to add a partner. At some firms, there wouldn't be enough clients to go around, so there may not be sufficient income to add another partner. Of course, if new partner candidates develop large enough client bases of their own, then there is usually no delay. Since 80-90% of *new* partners have yet to develop anywhere near a full client base on their own, this "business" reason for the long wait often prevails.

A "Be like Mike" issue? Average partners at typical local CPA firms are in their early 50s, manage over $1M of clients, have 20-25 years of solid experience, are very street-smart and earn over $400,000 per year. At many firms, the existing partners want new partners to be like them— an awfully high standard for new partners to meet.

Why am I raising this issue? I bring this up because the traditional model of operating a CPA firm is crumbling and that model has driven away many young, highly skilled staff unwilling to wait until their mid-30s or later to make partner.

The fallacy in the "business reasons" for taking so long to make partner. The problem doesn't lie with the new partners failing to qualify for a partnership. The real problem is that many existing partners don't perform two critically important partner duties *themselves*: bringing in business and developing young people into leaders. Let me explain.

At well-managed larger firms, clients are serviced with a firm, not an individual, orientation. Partners are expected to bring in new business continually. They are not allowed to coast once they build up a $1M+ client base.

When people are promoted to partner, many of the clients they serviced as a manager become their client responsibility. Also, other partners may transfer clients to new partners to build up their client responsibility. These two actions, combined with the new partners' own origination, result in an overall client responsibility amount that is respectable for a first year partner.

What happens to the existing partners who "lose" clients when new partners are made? As true partners, they are now responsible for bringing in new business to replace the clients they transferred.

This process has two system requirements. First, the firm must track business originated *(Finding)* separately from client responsibility *(Minding)* for each partner. At many firms, the Finder and the Minder for a given client are often different people. Second, the firm's partner income allocation system must be sophisticated enough to avoid (1) unfairly penalizing partners who transfer clients to others for the good of the firm and (2) granting windfalls to new partners who are the fortunate recipients of client transfers.

A complementary process is the use of a non-equity partner position as a middle step between manager and equity partner. This non-equity partner slot becomes a partner-in-training position. It will prepare personnel to handle a large client base and help partners evaluate their ability to handle it successfully. Once they become proficient, they may be elevated to equity partner.

With these systems in place, it becomes easier to offer partnerships to star managers at a much earlier age.

Shorten the Path to Partner

Firms should take a serious look at their systems and criteria for making someone a partner. For the vast majority of partner-potentials, it doesn't take 13-20 years to develop the skills and personality to function as a partner. Shortening the path will go a long way toward retaining the best and the brightest because (a) they see an opportunity for rapid advancement, (b) the firm recognizes their strong skills and personality traits and (c) they are well positioned for a dramatic increase in compensation.

Path to Partner Milestones Checklist

Milestones for Bringing in New Partners	Who?	Timing / Frequency
1. Talk about benefits of partnership.	Partners talk to partner candidates.	Start at staff level, add depth throughout career.
2. Discuss future leaders of the firm.	Partner group.	Ongoing (at least annually).
3. Develop leadership skills.	All.	Start at staff level, add depth throughout career.
4. Gauge interest in joining partnership.	Partners ask partner candidates.	Manager level, ongoing.
5. Develop specific partner-level skills (e.g. business development, organizational leadership).	Partner candidates.	Manager or senior manager, ongoing.
6. Explain role and expectations of partners at your firm.	Partners talk to partner candidates.	Senior manager.
7. Explain financials of partnership and buy-in (using realistic, estimated numbers for your firm).	Partners talk to partner candidates.	Senior manager.
8. Identify specific managers and senior managers with partner potential.	Partner group.	Ongoing (at least annually).
9. Evaluate fitness for partnership.	Partner group.	As needed for specifically identified partner candidates.

10. Define timeline for adding new partners.	Partner group.	Ongoing (at least annually), plus specific timelines once a candidate is likely to be offered admission.
11. Vote on offering partnership to identified candidates.	Partner group.	As needed.
12. Present partnership offer.	Partner group.	As needed.
13. Sign partnership offer.	Partner candidate.	Within ___ days of presentation of offer.
14. Celebrate joining partnership.	All.	As needed.
15. Set goals and expectations for new partner.	New partner + experienced partner.	At least annually.

5

Expectations of New Partners: To Help Staff Learn and Grow

Firms have two levels of expectations of new partners. Many firms aren't consciously aware of these alternatives, but they exist nonetheless, and they are quite different from each other.

Expectation 1: The new partner *is* qualified for the job.

New partners must drive the firm by

- Increasing revenue by bringing in new clients.
- Retaining clients and expanding services to them.
- Developing staff, helping them learn and grow.
- Providing proactive, world-class service to clients.
- Having the leadership skills to take over the firm from existing partners.

If new partners don't do these things, then they don't fully perform like partners.

Expectation 2: We hope the new partner *will become* qualified for the job.

When they promote staff, some owners hope the new partners will magically acquire partner-level skills. But often the new partners are best suited for retaining the status quo and simply aren't capable of driving the firm.

A few weeks before writing this, I started working with a small firm that was fortunate to have two managers meeting the requirements for partner. In the MP's words: "They are rock-solid and already performing at a partner level." *This is what every firm should want!*

This chapter is written from the following perspectives:

- The firm chooses the first of the two alternatives for new partner expectations.
- Staff are just as important as clients. The partners don't just *say* it. They *act* on it.
- Every generation of partner, from experienced to brand-new ones, is responsible for developing the next generation of partners.

The remainder of this chapter is excerpted from our book *CPA Firm Staff: Managing Your #1 Asset.*
https://rosenbergassoc.com/product/cpa-firm-staff-managing-your-1-asset/

Mentoring to Help Staff Succeed and Advance

"The delicate balance of mentoring someone is not creating them in your own image but giving them the opportunity to create themselves."
Steven Spielberg

The old-school attitude of developing staff is that they should pull themselves up by their own bootstraps. Partners are available to answer questions, but staff must *always* take the initiative.

The new-school attitude is for partners and managers to be proactive in developing staff. It should be a badge of honor (also handsomely compensated) for a partner or manager to be given credit for staff advancing under their tutelage and sponsorship.

Here are the most important things that partners and managers do to perform as great mentors:

1. Provide a safe place for staff to vent their true feelings, to ask questions, to seek guidance, to confide in you.

2. Advise staff how to advance in the firm and *proactively* help them along the way. Formal written goals should be set and monitored.

3. Focus on being a good listener, not a preacher or lecturer.

4. Mentoring must be done continuously, not just once or twice a year in formal, stiff meetings to meet a firm requirement. Mentors get to know what their protégés are like outside of work as well as professionally.

Performance Feedback

"Average players want to be left alone. Good players want to be coached. Great players want to be told the truth."

Doc Rivers
NBA Basketball Coach

"Good employees make mistakes. Great leaders allow them to."

Amy Rees Anderson
REES Capital, Managing Partner

The best book on management I have ever read was written 20 years ago. *The One Minute Manager* by Ken Blanchard and Spencer Johnson focuses on performance feedback. It's also about how to be a great mentor. New partners should read this book carefully and practice it every day.

Here are the three secrets of *The One Minute Manager.* Each of them takes only one minute to put into practice.

1. One-minute goal setting. Make it clear what the responsibilities are and what the subordinate is held accountable for. It should take no more than a minute to read each goal.

2. One-minute praisings. Give clear feedback on how staff are doing. Praise people immediately, giving specifics. Catch people doing something right. People who feel good about themselves produce good results.

3. One-minute reprimands. Give clear feedback on when staff do something that fails to meet expectations. Be specific. Give feedback that communicates unhappiness with the results; don't attack staff personally. Reassure them that you think well of them and that you value them as employees.

Continuous feedback ALWAYS trumps annual reviews. Continuous feedback means that when a project is completed, regardless of how short or easy it may be, the staff are given immediate feedback on their performance. This way feedback is fresh and can be used by the staff to immediately improve their performance on the very next project.

Most supervisors and their subordinates hate annual performance reviews. Why? Because (a) there often has been little or no feedback for an entire year, so when ancient history is dredged up, it surprises the subordinate; and (b) the session mostly looks *back* instead of forward. Both parties to the review are anxious and awkward. There *is* a role at firms for annual reviews, but only if there is continuous feedback during the year and the review session looks forward.

The annual session should provide guidance in these areas: What does the employee need to work on? What are his or her goals for the coming year? What does the person need to do to advance?

Leadership Development

Jack Welch was the long-time, highly successful CEO of General Electric. He said: "Before you are a leader, success is all about growing yourself. When you become a leader, success is all about growing others." The #1 factor in evaluating the performance of division presidents reporting to Welch was their success at developing leaders under them, even more so than profits.

This should be the credo of all partners, including new ones.

Here are the main ways CPA firms are developing their staff into leaders:

1. Mentoring, primarily by partners, but at larger firms managers are mentors as well.

2. Outside leadership development programs designed specifically for CPA firms. These programs are curriculum-based. They have multiple sessions, last from several months to two or three years and address a variety of subjects related to leadership.

3. Integrated with #1 and #2, staff are given client, staff and management opportunities to stretch their abilities and develop the talent to qualify for leadership positions in the firm, including partner.

Effective leaders develop skills in these areas:

Vision. A leader is always thinking about what the firm *should* be and regularly meets with other firms to share best practices.

Delegation. Leaders always err on the side of overdelegating to subordinates, stretching their abilities. New partners should avoid doing staff-level work. Work can always be delegated, but responsibility for ensuring that the delegated work is done correctly and on time can never be delegated.

People skills. Leaders treat people well and show empathy. They see people for what they *can* be. Great leaders understand that the #1 reason staff leave firms is their relationship with the boss, so they work hard to be great bosses.

Inspiration. Leaders introduce excitement and enthusiasm into the firm. This goes a long way toward *engaging* staff in the firm, a key to retention. This way, staff look forward to coming to work each day.

Conflict resolution. Leaders excel at conflict management and deal with problems promptly. When there are disagreements among partners on an issue, the worst thing a new partner can do is be neutral. New partners should get into the habit of taking positions on issues and influencing others. New partners should never avoid conflicts because they are new, afraid to criticize revered senior partners or easily intimidated.

Change. New partners play an important role in achieving change because their attitudes usually haven't become hardened and resistant to change. Understand what Roberto Goezueta, former president of Coca-Cola, said: "To succeed, we have to disturb the present."

Listening. Paying attention to what others say is the first act of respect and mutual support.

Accountability. Unless there are consequences when people fail to do what is expected of them, they will be less likely to achieve their goals or meet expectations. Good leaders hold others accountable in positive ways instead of wielding a club over their heads. Equally important, good leaders are always willing to be accountable *for their own* performance and behavior.

Communication. Good communication is all about talking ... clearly.

Charisma is vastly overrated and rarely seen among CPA firm partners. It's more important to be a leader with inspired *standards*.

Make the Staff's Work Challenging

The AICPA has conducted numerous surveys over the years about what is most important to CPA firm staff. Challenging work is always near the top of the list. (The other big ones are compensation and career growth opportunities and promotions.)

These are the things new partners and partner candidates can do to make staff's work challenging:

1. Stretch the staff's abilities. Resist the temptation to retain the more complex, challenging and "fun" work for yourself and instead delegate it to staff. Gradually give them more complex assignments.

2. Train staff to ask for more complex and challenging projects.

3. There is a natural reluctance to delegate complex work to someone who lacks the skills, knowledge and experience to do the work. Overcome this by taking the time to train staff to master these complex assignments.

4. Give your staff as much work variety as possible. This stretches their skills and helps them avoid doing the same things year after year.

5. Use technology, outsourcing and paraprofessionals to perform as much of the tedious work as possible.

Training

The CPA profession is technically demanding. When staff join a CPA firm, they have a unique opportunity to receive excellent compensation while obtaining rigorous, continuous training in their work. New partners and partner candidates are the main providers of this training and should passionately pursue this job requirement.

Here are training best practices:

1. On-the-job training is the most effective form of training for CPA firm staff, especially young people. It starts with the supervisor reviewing the engagement with the team before the job begins, clarifying expectations and giving specific instructions.

2. When a client project is complete, the supervisor should evaluate the performance of all team members. There should be a space on the client routing sheet for a sign-off that this was done.

3. Work should be reviewed in a timely manner. Supervisors should require the staff to make corrections themselves. Making corrections for them may be faster, but it won't teach the staff anything.

4. One-shot outside seminars need follow-up to be effective.

   a. Mentors should meet with staff after they have completed an outside seminar to help put to use what they learned. The firm should assign work to the staff person in the area that the outside seminar focused on.

b.   After a staff person returns from an outside training seminar, he or she should be required to present the highlights in a staff meeting. There is no better way to learn something than by teaching it.

5.   Use performance review and mentoring sessions to identify areas of future training for the person.

6.   Build training time into client budgets. You don't want a culture in which people avoid training younger staff because the budget doesn't allow for it.

7.   Lunch and learns. These are lunchtime, informal, small group sessions, often led by partners, on "business-thinking" subjects.

8.   The staff's work should be performed and reviewed in the field as much possible.

Recognizing and Rewarding Staff

One of my favorite lines from any source is from Mark Twain: "I can live on a good compliment two weeks with nothing else to eat." We all know how good it feels to do something and be told we did a good job on it. People often *say* they don't need this, but they are lying.

Here is an excerpt from a 2013 *Forbes* online article by Meghan Biro:

"People crave positive feedback and recognition when they put in extra effort. They love to be acknowledged by their leaders and peers and experience the glow that comes with knowing an achievement has been seen, appreciated and celebrated.

"Financial reward is a great thing, don't get me wrong, but it's not the equivalent of recognition. Let's not kid ourselves. It's a short-term solution. Neither is constant praise for average work. Recognition is a key tool in developing and retaining staff for a reason: people need more than constructive feedback and positive affirmation. They need recognition of extra effort. They need to 'feel' it. This will always be a basic human need."

Biro continues: "An effective approach to employee recognition encompasses these key points:

1. **In the moment.** Be timely. Catch people doing exemplary work and acknowledge their efforts. But don't just knee-jerk—showing up for work on time does not count in most cases.

2. **Appropriate in volume and scale**. Randomness is not your ally. Recognition should match effort and results or it loses meaning.

3. **Authentic, not automatic**. You have to mean it when you give staff recognition. The human touch is so important to effective recognition.

4. **Tied to the employee's perception of value.** Monetary rewards can skew this notion of value, linking it to cash when it should be linked to appreciation of extra effort and smarts. Money is appropriate much of the time, but it's not the only—or even the most effective—motivator. Treat employees as valued team members, not as numbers. Most of the time it's the best way to really recognize a valued player."

Common Ways CPA Firms Recognize Their Staff

1. Face-to-face praise always has been and always will be the best way to recognize people.

2. Provide public recognition at staff meetings and other firm events.

3. Hand out gift certificates or other awards.

4. Send thoughtful notes to individuals, with copies to MP, personnel file, etc.

5. "You've been working really hard. Take the rest of the day off."

6. Give promotions.

7. Award merit-based raises and bonuses.

8. Communicate above-average promotion potential in counseling and mentoring sessions.

9. Give recognition on the staffer's anniversary of service.

10. Mention the person's accomplishments in your internal newsletter.

59

Let's face it. CPAs are trained to identify problems, to find things that are wrong. Unfortunately, many firms' cultures take on this characteristic. Their attitude is "You get feedback only if you do something wrong." or "If you don't hear anything from me, that means you're doing well."

Don't let this happen on your watch!

6

A Crash Course in the Business of Public Accounting

The material in this chapter is from our book *How CPA Firms Work: The Business of Public Accounting.*
https://rosenbergassoc.com/product/how-cpa-firms-work-the-business-of-public-accounting/

"Engaging your employees—involving them in the business—can drive revenue growth. An educated workforce can also make better decisions, work more efficiently, and seize opportunities faster. Teaching your employees to be smart businesspeople can be a big investment, but it's one that can have a significant return."

Keith Lamb, *Inc.* magazine

Personnel in *any* organization, from widget manufacturers to hospitals to baseball teams to charities, work with more enthusiasm and commitment when they genuinely feel part of the organization. When people understand how they fit into the overall scheme and what their role is and grasp the essentials of how the organization operates, they produce higher quality work and are more energized. CPA firms are no exception to this rule.

The messages of this chapter:

- Partners should be *formally* educating their staff on the business of public accounting, how firms are structured, what makes them successful, how firms are managed, how they get clients, what makes them profitable and how profitability is held back.

- Staff who aspire to become partners should understand all of the topics listed above. If the firm doesn't proactively offer this education, then they should take it upon themselves to acquire this knowledge.

Services Provided by CPA Firms

CPA firms typically provide three main types of services, with each service having several subgroups. The mix of these three main services is shown on the next page, broken down by size of firm:

- Big 4 (Deloitte, PwC, Ernst & Young and KPMG)

- Large regional firms. These are roughly the largest 50 firms in the U.S. beyond the Big 4. Though an increasing number of these firms have become quasi-national firms, most are regional, based in the Northeast, Midwest, Southeast, Southwest, or another region. The 50th largest firm in the country has annual revenue of roughly $100 million.

- Local firms. These are multipartner firms below the regionals. Most have one or two offices.

Primary Services Provided by CPA Firms

	Big 4 (1)	Top 100 Firms (2)	Local Firms $2-$20M (3)
1. Audit and accounting:			
a. Audits & reviews	41%	30%	26%
b. Compilations, book- keeping, payroll, etc.	2%	7%	14%
TOTAL A&A (Note 6)	**43%**	**37%**	**40%**
2. Tax:			
a. Corporate/business	21%	24%	29%
b. Individual/1040s	4%	12%	18%
TOTAL TAX (6)	**25%**	**36%**	**47%**
3. Consulting (4):			
a. Specific areas (4)	28%	20%	4%
b. Handholding, misc. (5)	4%	7%	9%
TOTAL CONSULTING	**32%**	**27%**	**13%**

(1) From Big4careerlab.com.
(2) From IPA National Benchmarking Report.
(3) From The Rosenberg MAP Survey.
(4) See the next page for a list of the most common types of consulting.
(5) The term "handholding" is colloquially used to describe arguably the most important work that CPAs do for their clients. CPAs are their clients' most trusted advisors. Clients seek advice from them in a wide variety of areas, such as estate planning, paying for college, getting a business loan, hiring a controller, buying a company, investing their money, choosing what kind of insurance to buy ... The list is endless.
(6) The totals for the three primary services were from the sources listed above. Rosenberg estimated the breakdown within each service line.

Common Consulting Services and Industry Practice Areas

Data is from the IPA National Benchmarking Report, *Accounting Today* Top 100 Survey and The Rosenberg MAP Survey.

Consulting

Business valuations
Estate and financial planning
Litigation support
Forensic services
Retirement plans
Employee benefits
Technology consulting, including cybersecurity
Investment advice
CFO outsourcing

Industry practice areas

Real estate
Construction
Technology
Wholesale/distribution
Professional services
Nonprofits
Health care
Hotels and restaurants
Governmental
Retail
Entertainment
Financial institutions/banking

Common Position Titles at CPA Firms

Titles	*Most* Commonly Found at Local Firms	Some Firms Also Have These Positions
Entry level: staff assistant	• Recent accounting graduate. • Newly hired.	
Staff	Most firms don't have separate titles for these first two positions.	Has completed first year but is not yet a senior; does little supervising of other staff.
Senior	• First major promotion. • A senior performs most of the detailed work on a job. • Works one job at a time. • Supervises other staff. • Has lots of contact with partners.	
Super-visor		Intermediate promotion from senior but still below manager.
Manager	• On track to be a partner **or** it's a permanent position for highly experienced staff. • Common to work on several jobs at the same time. • Heavy supervision of staff. • Heavy contact with partner.	
Senior manager		Promotion from manager but still below partner.
Non-equity partner	Roughly 60% of all firms now have this position, though it's much more common at larger firms than smaller firms.	• Has most of the skills to become an equity partner. • Is often a partner in training. • Has heavy client relationship duties. • Is not an owner.
Equity (or full) partner	Highest position in the firm. An owner. Has final responsibility for all client matters.	

The U.S. CPA Firm Market

There are roughly 44,000 CPA firms in the United States. The market is skewed significantly from large to small:

- The Big 4 international firms (Ernst & Young, KPMG, PwC and Deloitte) account for 46% of the industry's total revenue.

- There is a huge fall-off from the Big 4 to the next tier of firms: The smallest Big 4 firm is five times the size of the fifth biggest firm.

- The 200 largest firms account for 65% of the industry's total revenue.

- The vast majority of the 44,000 firms are very small; most employ well under ten total people.

- Roughly 30,000 of the 44,000 firms are sole practitioners. Most are one-person operations but many have several employees.

The demographics of the 44,000 firms are summarized in the chart on the next page.

U.S. CPA Firm Market Demographics

	Number of Firms	Total Market Size (Billions)		Average Annual Revenues	Range of Annual Revenue
		Amount	Pct.		
The Big 4	4	$57.0	46%	$15B	$9B-$20B
#5-100	96	$20.0	16%	$212M	$40M-$2B
TOP 100 SUBTOTAL	100	$77.0	62%		
#101-200	100	$3.3	3%	$33M	$25M-40M
#201-300	100	$2.0	2%	$20M	$15M-25M
TOP 300 SUBTOTAL	300	$82.3	67%		
Next 2,000	2,000	$15.0	12%	$7M	$2M-$15M
Very small multipartner firms	11,700	$17.6	14%	$1.5M	Almost all under $2M
Sole practitioners	30,000	$9.0	7%	$0.3M	Almost all under $1M
GRAND TOTAL	44,000	$123.9	100%		

Data from Statistics.com, INSIDE Public Accounting, The Rosenberg Survey and author's industry knowledge. Excludes payroll companies.

I am unaware of any authoritative, exact source for the revenue size of the 44,000 CPA firms. The above is a very good guess. However, the point of the chart is to show how a relatively small number of firms dominate the market in terms of revenue. 300 firms comprise 67% of the market.

CPA Firm Economics 101

The Economic Structure of a CPA Firm

One of the main purposes of this book is to provide future CPA firm leaders with an understanding of how their firm operates as a business, including how it makes money and what holds back profitability. With this knowledge, team members will make better decisions about how they spend their time and perform their work.

All businesses have economic structures unique to their industries:

- Grocery stores are high volume, low profit margin.

- Real estate ventures use accelerated depreciation and other tax angles to generate cash flow and healthy ROIs.

- Professional sports teams focus on increasing the value of the franchise so it can eventually be sold for a gigantic profit.

The typical CPA firm is a **low-volume, high-priced business**, with a relatively high profit margin (generally 30-45% of revenue).

- The supply of CPAs relative to the demand for them is fairly low. This is due to the high level of technical knowledge required to become a CPA and a long-time decline in the popularity of a career in accounting. Most young people do not perceive the accounting profession as exciting. The result is a shortage of labor. This has led to firms operating at lower volumes than they would prefer, but it puts them in a position of charging strong prices.

- CPA firms enjoy their high profit margin due to a few interrelated factors. First, due to a shortage of staff at the senior and manager levels, partners are forced to perform more billable client work than they would like to or should do. Second, many CPA firm partners *enjoy* doing work that other firms would delegate to staff, which partly accounts for their lofty billable hours (often 1,200 to 1,400). Third, many CPA firm partners feel that a good way to increase their compensation is to work harder themselves and employ fewer staff.

The vast majority of a CPA firm's revenue is considered "annuity" business. Clients of CPA firms typically remain with their firms for five to 10 years or more, thereby providing a relatively safe revenue stream that continues every year, primarily for compliance projects such as audits, reviews, compilations, bookkeeping and tax returns.

Most expenses are fixed. Even though staff labor is theoretically a variable cost, with the exception of major recessions the head count at firms stays relatively constant despite fluctuations in revenue. Most firms can absorb a healthy number of new clients without increasing their personnel head count.

Also, due to the shortage of labor, most CPA firms are continuously in a hiring mode: If a firm is fortunate enough to come across someone who has a good resume and is available, the person will generally be hired immediately, even if the firm's revenue volume does not appear to justify increasing head count.

Low overhead expenses. CPA firms have low overheads compared to law firms and other businesses. Despite earning substantial profits, the vast majority of CPA firms are not big spenders. Many have very nice offices but would never be considered lavish. A very small percentage of a CPA firm's expenses are discretionary.

CPA firms are top-line driven. In the pursuit of increased profitability, many businesses must either increase revenues or decrease expenses. But CPA firms rarely focus on controlling expenses because there is little excess to trim. Instead, virtually focus is on increasing revenues.

CPA firms increase revenues by

- Bringing in new business and clients.

- Increasing billing rates.

- Increasing realization, billing a higher percentage of time spent on client work.

- Increasing productivity, getting personnel to bill more hours and work more efficiently.

Increases in revenue drop directly to the bottom line (profits) because these revenue increases rarely cause the firm's expenses to rise much.

Leverage is king. The vast majority of the work performed by a CPA firm is done by staff instead of partners. Therefore, one of the top operating strategies of firms is to maximize the amount of client work that each partner can create for nonpartners to perform, under their supervision. Achieving this high leverage frees up partners' time to devote to developing business, nurturing relationships with clients and referral sources and helping staff learn and grow.

Bigger is better. Any analysis of CPA firm profitability will consistently and conclusively show that the higher a firm's revenues, the higher its profits will be. This is because the bigger the firm, the more it can afford to invest in sophisticated marketing programs, develop specialties and niches, aggressively pursue mergers, create better training programs and hire high-level professionals in the administrative, marketing, HR and IT areas. All of these tactics attract larger clients (who pay higher fees), more talented staff and smaller firms looking to merge in.

Why Should Employees Care
How the Firm Makes Money?

The cynics among you might ask this question. After all, the profits that the firm earns from the staff's great work go directly into the partners' pockets, right?

70

What incentive do staff have to contribute to firm profitability? What's in it for them? Here are four good reasons:

1. Some of the profits flow directly to the staff in the form of higher salaries and bonuses. High levels of compensation enable the firm to retain its best people.

2. More money is available for career-enhancing training programs, updated technology, top-notch marketing and other niceties such as modern (not lavish) offices.

3. Capital is available to merge in smaller firms and attract larger and more sophisticated clients, creating new client opportunities for everyone, including the staff.

4. When a company's revenues and profits are increasing, a funny thing happens to office morale: Everyone is happier! Firm personnel are more fun to be with, more helpful and more willing to work together. Bosses are more patient and smile more often.

    The opposite of all those things happens when companies struggle. Ask anyone who has had the misfortune of working for a stagnant organization that struggles with profitability. It can be miserable.

Key Definitions

Charge hours or billable hours. A CPA firm's widgets (units of production) are hours. The vast majority of a firm's revenue is billed directly or indirectly by the hour, so CPA firms pay a lot of attention to the billable hours worked by their personnel.

Non-charge or nonbillable hours. All work time that is *not* worked on client projects. This includes training, firm meetings, business development, vacation, holiday and sick time.

Billing rate. All personnel, from partner to staff, are assigned standard hourly billing rates. These rates, when multiplied by the hours worked on client work, result in a number called **gross fees or billable time,** which eventually is billed to clients.

Timesheet. All charge and non-charge hours are recorded on time-sheets. These charge hours are entered into the firm's billing system and accumulate in the firm's work-in-process, which is the starting point for generating client invoices.

Work-in-Process (WIP). WIP is a receptacle in the time and billing system where all time and expenses are accumulated by client. When clients are billed part or all of the accumulated WIP, these billings reduce the WIP balances, leaving a net unbilled amount for each client. These amounts are either carried forward to subsequent months to be billed at a later date or written off.

Write-offs. CPA firms (law firms, too) are rarely able to bill for 100% of their actual time spent on client work. The amount of client work that is not billed to clients is written off. The vast majority of firms write off 10-20% of their client time.

There are many reasons for write-offs, including:

- Project inefficiencies that cannot be passed on to clients.
- Discounts given to clients to procure the engagement.
- On-the-job training. Experienced personnel often use client engage-ments to teach less experienced staff how to perform their work. This training often cannot be billed to clients.

Realization percentage. The percentage of all client work that is billed to clients. The realization percentage for most CPA firms is in the 80-90% range.

Billings are the actual amount of billable time that is invoiced to clients. The difference between gross fees (the value of *all* time worked on client projects) and billings (sometimes called net fees or net revenues) is write-offs.

Leverage. This term is used in many industries and has a different meaning in each of them. In CPA firms, there are two interrelated ways to define leverage:

- A partner delegating client work to a staff person. The more staff that each partner can keep busy with client work, the more the firm is considered leveraged.

- Leverage is measured as follows: If a firm has 5 equity partners and 25 professional staff (administrative staff are not included in the leverage computation), the staff-partner ratio is 5:1. Staff-partner ratio is a principal way that CPA firms measure leverage.

Income per partner. The total earnings of all equity partners divided by the total number of equity partners. IPP is the primary measure of a CPA firm's profitability.

The Four Most Important Metrics Used to Manage Profits

These four metrics are key to any analysis of CPA firm profitability.

1. **Fees per equity partner.** The firm's billings divided by the number of equity partners. This is one of the ways we measure leverage. The more billings each partner can manage, the higher the firm's profit margin. On average, partners do 10-15% of all work performed for clients; the remaining 85-90% is performed by staff under the partners' supervision. The higher the percentage of client work the partners perform, the harder it is for them to find the time to build their client base and help the firm achieve a high fees-per-partner ratio. To manage a large client base properly, partners need to delegate as much of the client work as possible to staff.

2. **Fees per person.** This is another leverage metric. The "person" part of the calculation is every employee in the firm, including administrative people. Firm head count is measured in full-time equivalents (FTEs). Someone who works 1,000 hours a year is considered a 0.5 FTE. One who works 1,200 hours a year is a 0.6 FTE. No one can ever be more than a 1.0 FTE, regardless of how many overtime hours they work.

3. **Staff-partner ratio.** This leverage metric. It is the number of professional staff (all client service staff who are not equity partners) divided by the number of equity partners.

4. **Billing rates**. The rates assigned to each person in the firm that are multiplied by charge hours to arrive at billings.

Many years ago, a great and very successful managing partner told me that the key to CPA firm profitability is "leverage and rates," epitomized by these four metrics.

A Typical CPA Firm Income Statement

	Amount	Percentage of Net Fees
Gross fees	$5,000,000	
Write-offs	500,000	
Net fees or billings	4,500,000	100.0%
Expenses:		
Staff salaries and benefits	2,000,000	44.4%
Overhead expenses*	1,000,000	22.2%
Total expenses	3,000,000	66.6%
Total income to the equity partners	$1,500,000	33.4%

* Rent, office supplies, marketing, insurance, training, IT costs, etc.

Examples of How Various Actions Impact a CPA Firm's Profits

Assume a firm with 8 partners and 28 professional staff.

1. **Everyone in the firm records only one *extra* billable hour per week.** Notice I said "records," not "works" an extra hour. Both partners and staff perform hundreds, if not thousands, of hours on client work that are recorded as nonbillable time instead of billable time. Why? It could be sloppiness in keeping track of time. Or perhaps someone feels guilty about spending too much time on a task. Maybe a manager spends a couple of hours training a staff person on a client engagement and makes a unilateral judgment that the time shouldn't be billed to the client. In many cases, this extra time *can* be billed to the client. But if the time never makes it to the billings records, it will never be billed.

   - One hour x 48 weeks per year, x 36 people = 1,728 hours
   - @ blended billing rate of $130, additional revenue=$225,000
   - @90% realization, $203,000 of additional profits.
   - No additional expenses should be incurred.

2. **18 people each bring in a $5,000 client.** Assume that half of the 36 client service personnel were able to bring in *just one* $5,000 client per year.

   - 18 people x $5,000 each = $90,000 of new revenue.
   - At 35% incremental profit, that equals $59,000 per year.

   If the client averages a 10-year tenure with the firm, the present value at 5% per year of bringing in this revenue is $300,000.

3. **18 people each lose a $5,000 client.** The reverse of #2. If half of the client service personnel in the firm provided such poor service to a client that the client left the firm, the cost to the firm over 10 years would be $300,000.

4. **The firm invests time in staff training.** Assume that managers and partners make the effort to spend more time training staff so that each staff person, on average, becomes able to bill one additional hour per week.

- One hour x 48 weeks x 28 staff x $100 per hour = $134,000.

- @ 90% realization = $121,000.

- If training time cost $25,000, incremental profit = $96,000.

5. **Partners push down work to staff and use the freed-up time to bring in new clients.** Assume the 8 partners delegate 100 billable hours each, per year, to staff. Further assume that the 800 hours of freed-up time is used for business development and that the result of those efforts adds $400,000 of revenues.

If the partners' billing rate is $250 and the staff's blended rate is $110, that's a difference of $140 per hour. If 800 hours of work previously billed by partners is now billed by staff, revenue will be reduced by $112,000.

- New business $400,000
- Reduced partner hours   112,000
- Profit increase $288,000

It's important to note that the firm should not reduce billings to clients simply because work formerly done by partners is now being done by staff at a lower billing rate.

6. **The staff is not very productive.** Assume that the firm's 28 staff average a disappointingly low 1,400 billable hours per year. If the firm can improve the staff's productivity by increasing the average from 1,400 billable hours to 1,600, a very realistic goal, the firm can make do with 24 staff instead of 28.

- Saving the cost of four people at $80,000 each (includes benefits) = $320,000.

Benchmarking Norms for CPA Firms

Annual Fees	Fees per Partner	Fees per Person	Staff Ptnr Ratio	Ptr Billing Rate	Income per Partner	Bill Hours Ptnrs	Bill Hours Staff
$2-5M							
2019	$1,136,669	$184,842	4.4	303	$345,537	1,163	1,448
2018	$1,031,407	$179,102	4.0	295	$332,717	1,137	1,409
2017	$1,045,286	$172,986	4.1	289	$334,615	1,149	1,445
$5-10M							
2019	$1,535,836	$190,269	6.0	329	$477,941	1,148	1,472
2018	$1,527,333	$178,746	6.2	318	$445,604	1,156	1,510
2017	$1,491,828	$178,533	6.3	311	$422,073	1,159	1,497
$10-20M							
2019	$1,895,655	$192,214	7.4	355	$506,375	1,043	1,493
2018	$1,813,824	$183,906	7.3	343	$479,451	1,028	1,486
2017	$1,773,257	$176,069	7.5	339	$473,320	1,022	1,480
> $20M							
2019	$2,543,042	$204,616	9.3	406	$674,711	1,031	1,474
2018	$2,339,067	$200,610	8.7	405	$643,170	1,034	1,448
2017	$2,123,735	$199,390	7.9	403	$634,949	1,056	1,469

Source: The 2020 Rosenberg MAP Survey. Data is for 2019.

The term "partner" here denotes "equity" partner.

The main takeaway from this chart is that generally speaking, the larger the firm, the stronger the performance, especially in profits, as indicated by the Income per Partner metric.

7

How CPA Firms Are Managed

Two Kinds of Firms

The first kind of firm argues that there is not much that *needs* to be managed at a CPA firm. These cynics might say: "Come on. Running a CPA firm isn't rocket science. You hang out your shingle. You get clients. You hire staff. You do the work. Bill and collect. What needs to be managed?"

Unfortunately, many CPA firm partners think this way—maybe not consciously, but it has the same effect. When firms learn that the lack of commitment to firm management shown by this attitude creates problems, they often hire consultants like me to help them address these types of issues:

- Staff turnover is high.

- Partners work like Lone Rangers; no teamwork.

- Computer systems are unreliable.

- Partners complain that the firm never has enough staff and definitely doesn't have *the right* staff.

- Bills go out late and are collected even later.

- The firm's policies and procedures vary, sometimes greatly, according to which partner you ask.

- Revenues and profits stagnate and disappoint.

The second kind of firm understands that CPA firms are just like other businesses. For them to be successful, these areas must be actively and effectively managed:

- **Human resources:** Staff must be recruited, trained and supervised effectively in order to provide partners with competent support.

- **Marketing and business development:** Clients aren't low-hanging fruit waiting to be picked from trees. Bringing in clients is extremely difficult for most CPAs. To be successful at it, the firm needs a marketing plan and accountability for business development.

- **Systems and technology**: Computers have revolutionized how CPAs' work is done. These days, if the firm's power goes out, people have to go home; that's how much they rely on their computers. Providing the firm with current technology and the systems that go along with it requires a substantial management effort.

- **Administrative duties:** If partners must routinely tend to the myriad of administrative tasks required to run a firm, their available time to bring in business, do client work and mentor the staff is greatly reduced. They need competent, experienced people like firm administrators, marketing directors, HR specialists and IT directors to keep the firm operating on a day-to-day basis.

- **Managing partner**: And finally, to ensure that all of these tasks are done expertly (and prevent the partners from killing each other), the firm needs *someone* to serve as the leader. A managing partner usually fills this bill.

Overarching Philosophies for Managing a CPA Firm

Accounting firms generally gravitate to one or the other extreme in each of the following areas:

1. **Partnership vs. corporate style**.
   - The partnership style is very much a democratic style. All partners are involved in all decisions, large and small. They vote on everything. They split up the admin duties, so everyone does their share. No partner would ever be trusted to make important decisions for all partners.

   - Corporate style. A CPA firm is a business and needs to be managed like one. Partners should do two things: take care of clients and take care of staff. Leave the firm's management to professionals hired for this purpose. Very few votes are ever taken because authority for making most day-to-day decisions is vested with management, not the partners.

2. **A team vs. a bunch of Lone Rangers.** Teamwork is the belief that the firm can achieve more when people work together than separately. Lone Rangers generally work alone and achieve success mostly as a result of their own individual efforts.

3. **Core values vs. a lack of values**. Attitudes and beliefs define the firm's culture. Core values are what the firm stands for, what is held dear and what the partners believe in. The acid test of whether or not a firm truly has a set of core values is the extent to which transgressions are allowed. If partners are free to define their own core values and allowed to violate these values willy-nilly, then there really are *no* core values.

4. **Production vs. a strategic vision.** Most firms agree that strategic planning is important. Some never allow the pursuit of the strategic plan to be trumped by production (bringing in business and working billable hours). Others value production above all else, addressing strategic planning only when they have spare time.

What Needs to Be Managed?

Strategic planning	The firm is driven by a vision of what the partners would like it to look like in 5-10 years.
Productivity	• Keeping staff busy; formal scheduling of staff. • Achieving individual targets for charge hours. • Achieving standards for quality of work. • Using nonbillable time effectively.
Processes	Will the firm do its work the same way, regardless of who is in charge of the client project? Or will the firm allow each partner to do it their way? Examples: Doing an audit Doing a tax return Filing for an extension Doing a physical inventory Billing clients Filling out a timesheet
Administration	Renting office space Billing system & collections Internal accounting Insurance Paying bills Budgeting Office equipment Firm policies
Quality control	Creation of written policies and standards for doing audit, accounting and tax work. Includes procedures to test personnel's compliance with the firm's standards.
Human resources/ staff issues	Compensation Benefits Personnel policies Training Orientation Mentoring Feedback Promotions Recruiting/hiring
Marketing of the firm	Marketing is all the things that promote the firm and get name recognition. Examples: branding, brochures, direct mail, seminars, speeches, articles.
Technology	• A dozen or so CPA-firm-specific software programs • Security, privacy, client portals • Mobile devices, remote access

Organization Charts

Small Firm
2-5 Partners/6-20 People

Medium Firm
6-10 Partners/20-50 People

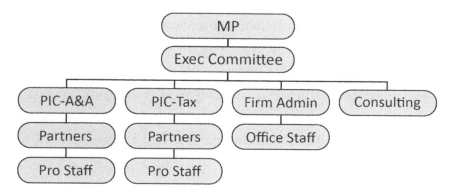

Large Firm
Over 10 Partners & Over 50 People

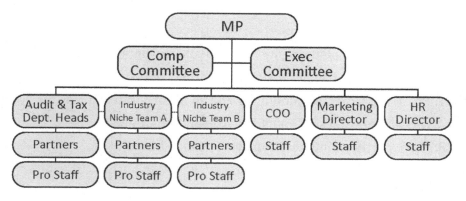

25 Best Practices of the Most Successful Firms

These 25 best practices have been extracted from my work with great firms over the past 20 years. Few firms do them all, but the best firms do most of them.

1. Pursue proactive business-getting efforts, with lots of team selling.
2. Exploit potential with existing clients.
3. Use the power of niche marketing and develop specialized expertise.
4. Provide world-class service.
5. Be a higher-priced, lower-volume firm.
6. Provide effective management, governance structure & leadership.
7. Franchise procedures.
8. Institutionalize client contacts; sell and service as a team.
9. Partners mess with clients and staff, staying out of administration.
10. Survey clients and staff to find out what they think of you.
11. Maximize staff-partner leverage. Partners are delegators, not doers.
12. Have a clear strategic plan. Vision. Direction. Implementation.
13. Get the right people ON the bus and the wrong people OFF the bus; create a common focus & culture.
14. Provide a diversity of services.
15. Tenaciously commit to making your firm a great place to work.
16. Make sure partners are good bosses so staff stay and get promoted.
17. Provide proactive leadership development.
18. Offer world-class training.
19. Do succession planning, including client account transition.
20. Maintain good partner relations; address conflicts.
21. Practice partner accountability and good corporate citizenship.
22. All partners and staff should have goals and targets.
23. Make partner compensation performance-based.
24. Put technology to work for you.
25. Benchmark to improve firm performance.

8

Key Concepts in Structuring a New Partner Buy-In

Two Major Benefits of Becoming a Partner

Accepting a partnership invitation offers two terrific, lifetime benefits to new partners that for most people cannot possibly be matched in any other career pursuit.

If they don't see this and agree with it, then perhaps it would be unwise for them to accept the partnership offer.

1. **The monetary benefit.** This consists of the substantial return on investment (ROI) of the new partner's initial buy-in (explained in the next section) as well as the outstanding compensation that partners in CPA firms earn compared to virtually all other jobs.

2. **The nonmonetary benefit.** This is just as important as the monetary benefit. Most people will spend more of their life working at their job than doing any other activity besides sleeping. So it makes sense that their job should be as enjoyable and satisfying as possible. The benefits of being a partner in a CPA firm include:

   - Having challenging work.

   - Helping clients you love and who love you.

- Being an entrepreneur in a small business.

- Feeling the satisfaction that comes with helping young people grow.

- Having staff to delegate work to, making it possible to focus on high-level priorities.

- Being your own boss, for the most part. Partners have a high degree of control over what they do, how they do it and when they do it.

- Working in an organization that has a diverse array of talent to draw upon, making teamwork a rewarding and enviable feature.

The Best Investment New Partners Will Ever Make

New partners make two major investments. The first is the initial buy-in at the outset of becoming a partner. The second is made over many years, sharing in the payment of buyouts of partners who retire or otherwise leave the firm. The burden of the latter is greatly lessened because it is shared with other partners in the firm.

The return on investment for new partner obligations is a whopping 23%. Here are the assumptions behind this calculation:

1. A manager is made partner at age 35.

2. The initial buy-in is $150,000, paid all at once.

3. The new partner joins five existing partners.

4. All partners, including the new one, retire at 65.

5. The new partner's share of buying out the five older partners, over the next 30 years, is $1 million.

6. The firm's annual growth rate over the next 30 years is 3%.

7. Compensation of the new partner starts at $175,000.

8. This compensation increases, on average, 7% per year.

9. If the new partner decides to quit and work in another job, their compensation would increase 2% a year. So, the assumption is that

a partner in a growing, profitable CPA firm will outearn all other jobs by 5% per year.

In addition, there's the appreciation of the initial capital investment and its return to partners upon their retirement. A $150,000 buy-in will appreciate to $364,000 in 30 years, assuming an annual increase of 3%.

All in all, the financial benefits of being a partner in a CPA firm are quite substantial. The money a new partner invests will probably be the best investment that person ever makes.

Create Written Criteria for Making Partner

Before shooting from the hip and elevating managers to partner because you somehow feel they are "ready" or have "earned it," think this through. Firms should *first* decide what experience, skills and achievements they want from a prospective partner *before* making the partnership offer. Firms should be consistent in applying this process. *Then* the firm should evaluate partner candidates against these criteria.

Here's another important reason to create *written* partner admission criteria: It's a critical part of the mentoring process. When partners talk to staff about their future with the firm and what it means to be a partner, it makes sense to share with them these written criteria.

These criteria were discussed in Chapter 3.

Consider the Non-Equity Partner Role *First*

For many years, local CPA firms have commonly promoted managers directly to equity partner for one or both of these reasons: (1) They intuitively felt that the manager earned the promotion or deserved it due to his or her excellent technical performance, loyalty as staff and years of service (time in grade) and (2) They made the promotion as a staff retention tactic, fearing that if they didn't, the employee would leave the firm, and that would give the partners heartburn.

As stated earlier, there is a trend well underway among CPA firms to raise the bar for becoming an equity partner. One reason for this is the increased use of the non-equity partner position.

Two common ways the non-equity partner position is used are:

1. As an equity-partner-in-training program. It gives the partner candidate one to three years to demonstrate that he or she is capable of functioning like an equity partner. The main skills to be demonstrated are managing client relationships, bringing in business and displaying leadership skills.

2. As a permanent position in the firm. This could be the case if the first type of non-equity partner is unable to acquire the necessary skills to advance to equity partner. Or it could be a manager who is unlikely to develop all the equity partner skills but deserves to be called a "partner" and is capable of performing many partner duties. The title is often advantageous for both employee retention and client-service marketing. Clients always want to know "Who's the partner?" on their account, and this person can fill that role and save an equity partner from having to keep the client.

The distinctions between non-equity and equity partners are described in great detail in Chapter 12.

Avoid Overemphasizing Ownership Percentage

The term "ownership percentage" has wrought havoc in CPA firm ownership structures for decades. Throughout my 20 years of CPA firm consulting, I have frequently asked partners to explain how their present ownership percentage was arrived at. Invariably, I'm greeted by blank stares. They don't have a clue.

Most CPA firms seem to feel it is intuitive to use ownership percentage to decide important financial and governance issues. Why is this? Firms reason: "If our clients do it, why shouldn't we?" Here are some reasons why they shouldn't.

Many companies derive a major portion of their growth, profitability, overall success and value from branded products, plant, equipment, proprietary processes, patented technology and the goodwill/market recognition that comes from these assets. It's understandable that an executive's ownership percentage in these businesses should impact financial and governance issues.

But CPA firms are different. Their primary asset is the partners' ability to bring in and retain annuity clients, *every day in every year*, to perform a highly technical service from scratch, *every day in every year* and thereby earn clients' trust and respect, *every day in every year*. The growth, profits and success of a CPA firm occur because of the quality of the owners' work effort and skills to create these benefits *every day in every year*. CPA firms need to reinvent themselves *every day in every year* to remain successful.

Relying too heavily on ownership percentage and not performance is a power grab and/or an opportunity to avoid accountability. It's so much easier to take 30% of the firm's profits because one is a 30% owner instead of *earning* it. It's so much easier to commit transgressions of firm policies (take excessive time off, be delinquent in billing and collections, give oneself a waiver on business or staff development) safe in the knowledge that one can never be held accountable for those short-comings due to the protection of a lofty ownership percentage.

One of the strongest arguments to minimize the importance of ownership percentage in CPA firms is simple: Fairness. It's simply not fair to rely on the use of ownership percentage to decide critical financial and governance matters. Heavy emphasis on ownership percentage is guaranteed to cause tremendous acrimony among current and future partners. Firms get twisted up in the illogic and unfairness of using ownership percentage and find themselves trying to solve problems that are unsolvable with old-school methods. They need to employ outside-the-box thinking.

Here is a simple illustration. Contrast the performance of the following two partners:

	Partner A	Partner B
Owner percentage	30%	20%
Business originated	$200,000	$500,000
Business managed	$800,000	$1M
Intangible performance	Average	Great

Can there be any possible justification for Partner A's compensation and buyout being 50% higher than Partner B's, simply because Partner A's ownership percentage is 50% more than Partner B's?

There are five major partner issues for which firms should resist determining their outcomes on ownership percentage. Here are recommended alternative treatments:

1. Allocation of partner income. It should be based primarily on each partner's performance, not their ownership percentages.

2. Calculation of partner buyout. It should be based primarily on what partners have contributed to the firm's profitability and success, usually measured by relative partner income, not ownership percentage.

3. Voting. It should be one person, one vote for the vast majority of issues (though most firms tell us they rarely take formal votes). If voting is based on ownership percentage, new and younger partners feel disenfranchised because older partners control the votes.

4. New partner buy-in. It should be determined as a fixed amount, independent of ownership percentage. Use of ownership percentage to determine new partner buy-in usually results in an enormous buy-in cost that new partners are unwilling or unable to pay.

5. Allocation of proceeds of a firm sale. It should use the same method as partner buyout. Why use ownership percentage for firm sales when you use performance-based measures to decide buyout? This makes no sense. They really are the exact same transaction.

New Partner Buy-In: Key Concepts

The value of a CPA firm. There are two components: Capital and goodwill, the latter of which is often stated as a percentage of the firm's annual revenue. Capital is on the balance sheet; goodwill is not.

Here's a crash course in CPA firm business valuations. Assume a firm with annual revenue of $10M. Most firms have accrual basis capital of roughly 20% of their revenues, consisting mostly of WIP and A/R. If we value the goodwill at 100% of revenue (this used to be so common it was automatic; today it is still common but much less so), the total value of the firm is $12M: $2M of capital and $10M of goodwill.

90

Why is this important? Because when new partners buy into the firm, they are purchasing a part of the total value of the firm, which is quite substantial.

The decline of large buy-ins. In the old days, a manager would be summoned to the MP's office and informed that he (and it was almost always a he) was being promoted to partner. While the manager was still wafting in the euphoria of finding out that he'd just been awarded the equivalent of a professor's tenure, the MP stated that the buy-in would be $600,000, preferably in $10s and 20s. Being of a generation raised to, when ordered to jump, dutifully respond, "How high?" he went home and figured out how to come up with the money.

How did the $600,000 get computed? The firm would first decide what ownership percentage to award the new partner. Let's assume that is 5%. This would be multiplied by the value of the firm, $12M, to arrive at $600,000.

At least 15 years ago, it became apparent to most firms that these enormous buy-ins were untenable. New partners were neither willing nor able to pay these buy-ins.

This old-school tactic was replaced by the following:

- The firm decides on a discretionary, fixed buy-in, enough for the new partner to have skin in the game, with a substantial amount of money at risk. The buy-in as of 2020 for most firms, large and small, is in the $100,000 to $175,000 range. Very small firms may have a buy in considerably less than $100,000.

- There is a disconnect between the buy-in and ownership percentage.

- The buy-in is usually paid to the firm by money withheld from the new partner's compensation over a period of years. Most firms try to make sure the net cash new partners take home is higher than their manager take-home pay.

As is the case with all major life changes, there are still some holdout firms that continue to require large buy-ins. But 95% of all firms have opted to make their new partner buy-ins affordable.

Performance-based compensation. The vast majority of all multi-partner CPA firms allocate income using a system that is performance based. A performance-based system is simply one in which partners' pay is in direct proportion to their performance compared to the other partners. The better one performs, the higher the pay. And vice versa. Systems that are *not* performance-based are primarily based on ownership percentage or pay-equal. In these systems, a partner's income is unaffected by performance.

Why is this important? New partners should understand that beginning on their first day as a partner, they will be paid based on how well they perform and how the firm performs. They aren't suddenly entitled to share in a huge profit pool without first *earning* it. Besides, if a new partner's income went way up, the way the math works, all the other partners' income would have to go down. But that doesn't sound very fair, does it?

No windfalls. Similar to performance-based compensation, the process of being promoted from manager to partner should not result in any windfall financial gains to the new partner. Most firms will give the new partner a nice promotion raise of perhaps 10-15%. That's it. No windfall.

Another windfall that new partners *do not* get. New partners don't receive ownership in the firm unless they pay for it. Let's go back to the example of the $10M firm. Buy-in practices have changed to requiring a relatively nominal buy-in, say, $150,000. But with this buy-in, new partners are not *buying* any of the value of the firm. If the firm was worth $12M before the new partner was admitted, the value of the firm after it receives the new partner's buy-in is now $12,150,000 (assuming the buy-in is paid immediately, all at once, as capital). That's it. If the new partner wants to pay, say, $600,000 to acquire part of the $12M value, the partners would probably be more than happy to accept the money.

The $12M value is relatively liquid. It has a reliably established value on the street. No one in their right mind would give it away for free or for a bargain price. New partners need to understand this.

Sweat equity. As you read the last paragraph, some of you may be wondering about sweat equity. This colloquial term means a new partner is gifted a percentage of the firm in recognition of years of devoted, excellent service to the firm, service that enabled the partners to service their clients and reap the financial benefits that come with this. Sweat equity is very rarely granted, but as with so many things, it's up to the partners of the firm what they want to do.

Voting. It's natural for partner candidates to look forward to having a vote once they become partner. It feels like an inalienable right that any owner in an enterprise should be entitled to.

Make no mistake about it: New equity partners do get a vote. But the significance of getting a vote is often much ado about nothing. Most firms take few, if any formal votes. Instead, they discuss and brainstorm issues at hand, reach a consensus and make decisions.

The real significance of a vote is to have a seat at the table or, as sung in the great musical *Hamilton,* "to be in the room where it happens." Each partner has the opportunity to *influence* other partners to agree with their own position. More often than not, as a practical matter, *that* is what constitutes a vote.

Assets of the firm. Clients and staff are assets of the firm, not of any individual partner or staff person. I once was engaged by a three-partner firm to help them devise a methodology for bringing in a new partner, something they hadn't done for quite some time. As part of this project, they asked me to explain to the partner candidate what it means to be a partner and the provisions of the firm's partner agreement. When we got to the nonsolicitation agreement, the manager shrieked with horror. Unbelievably, he said: "I'm not signing that agreement. In five years or so, I want to start my own firm and take some of the firm's clients I've worked on for years to get started." Needless to say, when the partners heard this, they terminated the manager.

It's important for new partners to understand that clients and staff are assets of the firm. Therefore, *no* firm members, including partners, are allowed to take these assets with them if they leave the firm. Well-managed firms require staff to sign nonsolicitation agreements and incorporate a nonsolicitation covenant in their partner agreement.

The enforceability of this provision in partner agreements is, for the most part, legally indisputable. The enforceability of nonsolicitation agreements for staff, on the other hand, is subject to state laws, which vary widely. Most nonsolicitation agreements provide for liquidated damages if they are violated.

9

How to Structure
the New Partner Buy-In

Let's go over structuring a new partner buy-in step by step.

Structuring a New Partner Buy-In

1. **Calculate the value of a CPA firm as accrual basis capital PLUS goodwill.** Goodwill is commonly expressed as a percentage of the firm's annual revenue. This total value should not be given away to anyone without being paid for. Bringing someone in as an owner in a profitable, viable business for little or no buy-in makes no sense.

2. **Define the criteria for making someone a partner.** The first step in bringing in a new partner should be for the firm to satisfy itself that the candidate meets its criteria. These are presented in Chapter 3 in a chart titled Bringing in a New Partner: Thresholds and Core Competencies. These criteria represent the best practices at the finest firms in the country.

Every item on the Thresholds chart is very important, but four stand out from the others:

a. Trust. The partner group should trust new partners to execute sound judgment in their conduct as partners. To be ethical and mindful of their obligation to protect the firm at all times. To always adhere to the firm's core values and policies. If you don't trust people to be your partner, you should never be partners with them, regardless of their strengths in areas that will benefit you financially, such as bringing in business.

b. Ability and willingness to take on the financial obligations of an owner. This mainly pertains to paying the new partner buy-in, sharing in the obligation to pay buyouts to departed partners and in general adhering to the provisions of the firm's partner agreement.

c. Credibility with clients and staff. New partners should have the executive presence to earn the respect and confidence of clients, especially when they take over client duties from a predecessor partner. Credibility also extends to staff; new partners should be seen by the staff as both earning and deserving of the partner position.

d. Bringing in business. As we have discussed throughout this book, the ability to originate clients is a controversial threshold for new partners. Some firms require it; others don't. One thing is for sure: *All* firms *prefer* that new partners have skills for bringing in business.

3. **Determine the buy-in.**

    a. **Few large buy-ins.** Many years ago, a new partner's buy-in was almost always determined by multiplying the newly awarded ownership percentage times the value of the firm (capital PLUS goodwill). Using this approach today results in buy-in amounts of hundreds of thousands of dollars at most firms, an amount young partners are neither willing nor able to pay.

    To structure the buy-in so it's affordable to the incoming partner, the firm has to *sever* the link between ownership percentage and the buy-in. This is simple: arbitrarily decide on a more affordable buy-in amount. Based on our work, the vast majority range between $100,000 and $175,000 for both large and small firms.

In a recent survey by The Rosenberg Associates, only 11 firms out of 348 set their buy-ins at $500,000 or more.

Virtually all the rest were $200,000 or less. If your firm wants to charge a huge buy-in to new partners, and they are willing to pay it, then that's your decision. But that barrier may limit your pool of qualified candidates.

The key is this: All partners in the firm should have a meaningful amount of their own money at risk, invested in the firm. People will act more like owners when they have *their own* money invested in the firm.

b. **How the buy-in is paid.** Virtually all firms work out an arrangement whereby the new partner pays the buy-in via a salary reduction. A common payback period is 5 to 8 years. Whatever the arrangement, it's important to ensure that new partners take home more cash than they did when they were managers.

c. **No guarantees**. If new partners choose to borrow money from a financial institution to pay the buy-in, firms do not guarantee the loans. Many years ago it was common for firms to make these guarantees, but firms long ago got out of the banking business.

d. **To whom the buy-in is paid**. At most firms, the buy-in is paid to the firm. At a minority of firms, almost always small firms with, say, two or three partners, we have seen new partners "buy" their ownership directly from existing partners.

Paying buy-ins to the firm instead of directly to partners is consistent with the one-firm concept and a best practice. Many problems are created when buy-ins are paid directly to individual partners:

i. Buy-ins arranged between two partners are outside of the control of the firm, counter to the one-firm concept.

ii. When new partners pay the buy-in directly to a current or retiring partner, it is often accompanied by the transfer of

97

the "giving" partner's clients to the new partner. This precludes the firm from being able to decide how to transfer clients in the best interest of the firm.

iii. If the firm uses a formula to allocate partner income, and the new partner is the recipient of a substantial client base, this will create a compensation windfall that is not fair to other partners.

iv. If ownership percentage is an important factor in determine-ing voting, compensation, buyout and other things, a buy-in handled between partners instead of firm-wide could alter the relative partner ownership percentages in ways that could be unfair to the firm's other partners.

v. More often than not, the terms of each buy-in differ from those of the last, which turns the buy-in process into a negotiated transaction that often is not in the best interest of the firm and almost always results in inconsistencies.

4. **Clarify what new partners get for their buy-in.** This is a question new partners ask, justifiably, when they are informed of the buy-in requirement. Firms should be prepared to respond.

a. First and foremost, new partners essentially get to be a member of the "club." They get to become owners of an organization that operates a highly profitable, growing, prestigious firm that will provide them with an income stream for 20 to 40 years that is well above what most people earn.

b. Many firms pay interest on partner capital accounts as a layer of the partner compensation system, often at percentage points above the prime interest rate. This, of course, applies only in cases where the firm's compensation system has a tier for interest on capital.

c. Partners get their capital back when they leave the firm.

d. They share in the value of the firm and its substantial increase in value over their decades as a partner. When they retire, they will receive a stream of payments that may total as much as three times their compensation.

e. They get the recognition of being a partner and, along with it, a say in how the firm is run and a vote on decisions.

5. **Eliminate the term "ownership percentage" from your vocabulary.** There should be no connection between the new partner buy-in amount and the person's ownership percentage. See Chapter 8 for more details.

6. **Determine partner compensation primarily by what partners contribute to the firm's growth, profitability and success each year.** This applies to new partners as well. The key is that the firm's partner compensation system should be performance-based. See Chapter 10 for more on this.

    Many firms award new partners a promotion raise, but it is relatively modest. The range of 10-15% is common.

    In the first several years after someone becomes a partner, many firms adopt an informal policy of erring on the side of being generous. This is an attempt to move the new partner's compensation up several notches.

7. **Account for capital.** Regardless of whether the firm is a corporation or a partnership, there is a substantial amount of accrual basis capital in a firm. Each partner owns some portion of that capital.

    There are several methods for determining how much capital each individual partner "owns." They are listed in order from most common to least common.

    a. The old-fashioned partnership accounting method. If the firm is a partnership, this is self-explanatory.

    b. Each partner's share of capital is in the ratio of his or her ownership percentage. This is inherently unfair because over time, ownership percentage ratios rarely correspond to how each partner performs relative to the others.

    c. Each partner's share of capital is in the ratio of his or her partner compensation. Two important caveats:

  i. The firm must have a performance-based partner compensation system, not a pay-equal system or one based on ownership percentage.

  ii. The partners must feel that the system and the results are reasonably fair (not perfect!).

 d. Corporations value the shares of stock owned by each partner, and that is how each partner's share of total capital is calculated.

A partner should never be allowed to withdraw capital except for purposes of death, disability, withdrawal or expulsion from the firm.

At most firms, there is a difference between their accrual basis income and the actual *cash* distributions made to the partners. The gap between the two is due to cash-flow considerations. The actual cash distributions should be in the same ratio as the income-sharing ratios determined by whatever income allocation system is adopted by the firm. In other words, partners should not be allowed to overdraw because they "need the money."

8. **Plan for goodwill-based buyout payments.** This is a major financial benefit of being an equity partner. When the partner leaves the firm by retirement, death, disability, withdrawal or expulsion, his or her interest in the firm is purchased by the firm. The payments are called partner buyout payments. Partner buyout alternative plans are discussed in Chapter 11.

9. **Understand what a new partner does NOT get.**

 a. A windfall.

 b. A huge promotion raise.

 c. Assets, unless the partner pays for them.

 d. A right to participate in the management of the firm.

 e. Waivers from being accountable for performance and behavior.

10. **Define what happens if the firm is sold or merged.** The proceeds of a firm sale should be allocated in the same way as if each partner

retired under the firm's partner buyout plan. Ownership percentages should *not* be used.

11. **Specify how the role of new partners changes from when they were managers.** See the last section of Chapter 3 for an explanation.

12. **Allow voting.** The importance of voting tends to be overstated. Firms rarely take votes. Instead, they discuss matters, reach a consensus and make a decision. So a vote is really more a right to sit at the decision-making table and influence others.

13. **Have a nonsolicitation agreement.** Well-written partner agreements prevent partners from taking clients and staff if they leave the firm. Most partner agreements provide liquidated damage penalties for doing so. New partners MUST sign this agreement.

14. **Consider a non-equity partner alternative.** Firms may not wish to automatically promote a manager directly to equity partner. Many firms promote their managers to non-equity partners and then have them meet more stringent requirements to become equity partners.

15. **Sign the partner agreement.** New partners must sign to formalize their admission to your firm's ownership ranks.

New Partner Buy-In Common Practices

Feature	Common Practices
1. Total value of the firm	Accrual basis capital + intangible (goodwill) value
2. Most important criteria for partner promotion	1. Trust. 2. Willingness and ability to take on retirement obligations. 3. Credibility with clients; executive presence to take over client relationships. 4. Often, bringing in business.
3. Buy-in	1. Set initially at $75-175K. 2. $10-20K down payment for some firms. 3. Pay buy-in via draw or salary reduction. 4. Pay over 5-8 years, making sure new partners' take-home pay exceeds take-home amount when they were managers. 5. If they get bank loans, no firm guarantees. 6. Buy-in is paid to the firm, not to individual partners.
4. What do new partners get for their buy-in?	1. Become member of the club, with substantial income stream for 20-40 years. 2. Interest on capital, if this is part of comp system. 3. Capital returned upon leaving the firm; increases as the firm grows. 4. Vesting in the value of the firm. 5. A vote (really more a seat at the table).
5. Ownership percentage	1. The term is used minimally in the firm. 2. Keep to a minimum the impact of ownership percent on (a) buy-in amount, (b) partner comp, (c) partner buyout and (d) voting.
6. Partner compensation	1. Ideally, new owner should receive a 10-15% promotion raise. 2. Make sure the system is performance-based. 3. Err on the side of being generous to new partners in the early years.
7. Capital	1. Use the partnership method of accounting for tracking the amount of each partner's capital. 2. No withdrawals of capital allowed. 3. Paid upon leaving the firm.

Feature	Common Practices
8. Goodwill-based payments at retirement/buyout	1. Though 1x fees is common, industry avg. = 80%. 2. Multiple of comp method is most common. AAV method works well if no previous plan.
9. What new partners do NOT get	1. Windfalls. 2. Assets that they do not purchase. 3. The right to participate in firm management. 4. A waiver on partner accountability.
10. If the firm is merged or sold	Allocation of proceeds is the same as if every partner did a normal retirement.
11. How the role of a new partner changes	1. May not change too much at onset. Depends on whether the firm can replace the manager role the new partner was occupying. 2. Many new partners take over clients worked on as a manager. 3. Bring in a new manager to free up new partners' time to function like partners. 4. Develop the leadership skills of managers. 5. Most firms expect new partners to actively bring in new business to *some* extent. 6. Many firms expect new partners to develop a niche or specialty service.
12. Voting	1. Most firms almost never take formal votes. 2. Reality: voting gives the new partner a seat at the table & opportunity to influence others. 3. Voting everything on ownership percentage "disenfranchises" the new owner. 4. One person, one vote for most matters. Several exceptions. 5. Founders must be protected from minority partners tossing them out.
13. Nonsolicitation agreement	New owner MUST sign a nonsolicitation agreement against taking clients and staff.
14. Non-equity partner alternative	Many firms require prospective equity partners to spend 1-3 years as NE partners before becoming equity partners. Serves as a training period and a time to see if the new partner is a good fit. Sometimes the non-equity position is permanent.
15. Partner agreement	Must sign.

Impact of Ownership Percentage on Partner Issues

Area of impact	Impact of ownership percentage	Explanation
1. Allocation of partner income	Minimal	• Probably at least 80% of partner income should be allocated based on performance. • Exception: interest on capital. • Some firms like to pay a segment of income equally or near equally to all partners. OK if the amount is *small*.
2. Retirement/ buyout payments to a departed partner	None	• Preferred partner buyout methods such as multiple of compensation or the AAV method have no component for ownership percentage. • Bulk of a partner's accumulated buyout should be considered deferred compensation and, as such, have a significant performance component.
3. Determination of buy-in amount	None	• Buy-in determined as a fixed amount at partners' discretion. • Buy-in amount has nothing to do with ownership percentage.
4. Voting	None	Most votes should be conducted on a one-person, one-vote basis on certain supermajority issues.
5. Sale of the firm	None	Proceeds to each partner should be based on relative accumulated retirement benefits.

Alternative New Partner Buy-in Methods

The method described earlier in this chapter is a CPA firm industry best practice. We have seen alternatives that some firms prefer, though each has disadvantages.

1. **All partners have equal ownership percentage.** This works great if the firm has minimized or eliminated the impact of ownership percentage, per the chart on the previous page.

2. **The firm arbitrarily determines a new partner's ownership percentage.** The buy-in is computed by multiplying the ownership percentage times the value of the firm. Some firms use a firm value that includes only capital, which can result in a reasonably sized buy-in amount. Others use capital plus goodwill, which usually results in unrealistically large buy-ins.

3. **Ownership percentage is periodically adjusted by the firm's management.** I see this only at very large firms. With this method, the firm's compensation committee adjusts partners' ownership percentage periodically based on their performance. Some percentages are increased, while others are decreased. Partners with increases must contribute more capital; those who experience ownership decreases have capital repaid to them.

   In this case, ownership percentage is really a way for the firm to allocate the most income to the higher performers and the least income to the weaker performers.

10

Partner Compensation

It would take a book much longer than this chapter to properly explain the finer points of partner compensation, especially how each of the major compensation systems works. Oh, did I forget? We wrote such a book, *CPA Firm Partner Compensation: The Art and Science.* https://rosenbergassoc.com/product/cpa-firm-partner-compensation-the-art-and-science/

Best Practices and Key Concepts

As is the case with all of my lists, no one firm incorporates *all* of these practices in its partner compensation policy. But I have observed *all* of the practices below in one or more of the best firms I've worked with over 20 years.

1. **Performance-based.** There should be a strong link between pay and performance. When it comes to CPA firm performance and profitability: As the partners go, so goes the firm. The partners have a much greater impact on the firm's success than professional staff and other personnel. If they perform at a high level, the firm will do the same. If partner performance lags, then the firm will suffer. Therefore, the firm needs to motivate the partners to produce at high levels and reward them accordingly. Compensation isn't the best way to motivate anyone's performance, but it *is* effective.

2. **Business getting.** Bringing in business must be a major factor in allocating partner income. BD is the most important aspect of partner performance that is also *the most difficult*. The majority of CPA firm partners are not highly skilled in BD. It doesn't come naturally to them. To be successful at bringing in business and contributing to the firm's revenue growth, most partners need to go outside their comfort zones. These efforts must be handsomely rewarded if firms expect their partners to make the extra effort to bring in business.

3. **Most important partner performance factors.** These are easily the biggest factors among many:

   - Bringing in business.

   - Managing the firm.

   - Providing world-class service to clients.

   - Managing a large client base.

   - Retaining clients and moving them upscale.

   - Helping staff learn and grow; mentoring them.

   - Intangible areas such as teamwork and loyalty.

4. **Multitier compensation systems.** Most firms adopt two or three tiers of income:

   a. Return on capital. This tier separates partners' roles as shareholders and producers. The core philosophy here is that shareholders have money invested in the firm and are entitled to a return on their investment. At most firms, this tier is 2-10% of total partner income.

   b. Base salary. This represents what each partner brings to the table every day. The base is primarily based on cumulative, historical performance, reflecting each partner's street value. At virtually all firms, this is by far the largest tier, usually 60-90% of total partner income.

   c. Bonus. This rewards unusually good performance in the current year. Whereas the base is a partner's street value, based a great deal on historical performance, the bonus is

"What have you done for the firm lately (this year)?" At most firms, the bonus is 10-30% of total partner income.

Firms treat the bonus in two distinctly different ways:

i.   The base is *independent* from the bonus.

ii.   The base is really a draw on a final income number; the bonus trues up the base to the final income number for each partner.

5. **Method for allocating income.** Firms use several methods **to allocate income**. The two most common are these:

   a.   Compensation committee. This panel of a small number of partners subjectively analyzes each partner's performance and links the performance to pay. This is the most common system by far at firms with eight or more partners. It's considered the Cadillac of all partner compensation systems because it's the best system for recognizing the critical importance of *both* production and intangible factors and it entrusts the income allocation process to a panel of judges that the partners trust to exercise good judgment and fairness in their deliberations.

   b.   Formula. The firm develops an algebraic formula for computing each partner's income. The main factors are pro-duction related: Finding (originating clients), Minding (managing client engagements and relationships) and Grinding (billable hours). Every formula must adopt a method of weighting the various production factors. Formulas are notoriously flawed for ignoring critically important intangible performance factors. They are most commonly used at firms with five or fewer partners.

6. **Goal setting.** There should be a link between pay and the extent to which partners meet their expectations. One of the best ways to measure this is with formal, written goal setting.

7. **Differentiation between management and administration.** *Management* is deciding what the firm should be and implementing. It's leading. It's holding others accountable for their performance and behavior. *Administration* focuses on the day-to-day running of

the firm. It monitors results, operates systems and supports practice personnel. Both are important, but management is much more valuable than administration. Most firms avoid paying partner-level compensation to do administrative work when the latter can be performed—usually more effectively—by someone earning a fraction of a partner's income.

8. **Teamwork.** Firms perform best when their partners work together as a team. They collaborate on clients. From time to time, clients are transferred from one partner to another when it's in the best interest of the firm.

9. **Originated book vs. inherited book.** It goes without saying that bringing in business is a critical performance factor. Managing client engagements and relationships is also very important, including situations where partners inherit clients that they did not originate (a partner retires or otherwise leaves the firm, new partners are assigned clients he or she worked on, etc.) In compensating partners, when a weight is assigned to managing clients, originated book should always be compensated more than inherited book.

10. **Partner evaluations.** There is a common myth among both partner candidates and partners themselves that once people become partners, they no longer need performance evaluations. Better firms say hogwash to this. The purpose of partner evaluations is to improve performance; partners need to improve their performance, just like staff. Partner evaluations should be used as a factor in allocating partner income.

11. **Partner accountability.** There are several ways to hold partners accountable for their performance and behavior. Compensation is probably the most commonly used accountability measure in CPA firms, though it is not always the best.

Seven Systems Used to Allocate Partner Income

The following chart shows the kinds of systems that firms across the country are using. The information is from a recent edition of The Rosenberg MAP Survey.

Seven Systems Used to Allocate Partner Income

System	2 Partners	3-4 Partners	5-7 Partners	8-12 Partners	13 + Partners	All Firms
Comp Committee	6%	12%	33%	57%	78%	33%
Formula	30%	33%	31%	18%	16%	27%
Paper & Pencil	3%	2%	5%	2%	0%	3%
Ownership Percentage	6%	4%	7%	5%	3%	5%
MP Decides	15%	17%	9%	13%	3%	12%
Pay Equal	27%	6%	0%	2%	0%	5%
All Partners Decide	12%	26%	14%	3%	0%	14%

Observations that can be drawn from the chart:

1. The compensation committee method is clearly the choice at the larger firm levels.

2. The formula is the most commonly used system at the smaller firm sizes. One reason for this is that the firm doesn't have enough partners to justify using a compensation committee.

3. Using ownership percentage to allocate partner income is not very common because it is inherently unfair: Only through a quirk of fate will partners' ownership percentages be in line with their relative levels of performance.

If your firm uses a formula, new partners will likely not fit into your system because most new partners have not built up their client base and other production metrics sufficiently to result in a reasonable compensation under the firm's formula. In many cases, trying to fit new partners into an existing partner compensation formula will result in reducing their salaries, which of course is unfair and inappropriate.

To address this dilemma, most firms continue to determine the new partners' compensation the same way as when they were managers. This means the compensation amount of new partners needs to be carved out of the formula system.

What Promotion Raise Should New Partners Receive?

The key concept is this: New partners should not receive a compensation windfall. They should receive an increase in pay that is

1. A reasonable or even slightly generous promotion raise because it IS a big promotion.

2. Sufficient to put their take-home pay higher than during their last year as a manager.

3. Recognition of what they are contributing to the firm's growth, profitability and success.

Most new partners receive an increase in the range of 10-15%. Firms find this is adequate to address the three issues above.

One final suggestion: Many firms I have worked with have a policy of erring on the side of being overly generous to new partners in their first few years as a partner. The objective is to get them up to a "healthy" compensation level relatively quickly. This practice is much more common at firms with well above average profitability levels because they make more money and can *afford* to be generous. It goes a long way toward making new partners feel better about their minority roles in the firm and more comfortable taking on the retirement obligations to come.

11

Partner Retirement/Buyout

This chapter summarizes key points that new partners should know about CPA firm partner buyout plans. If you want greater detail, you're in luck. We devoted an entire book to the subject, *CPA Firm Partner Retirement/Buyout Plans.* https://rosenbergassoc.com/product/cpa-firm-partner-retirement-buyout-plans/

One of the benefits that new partners receive in exchange for their buy-in is that they will receive a buyout when *they* retire. This amount can be in excess of a million dollars at many firms. Receiving a retirement buyout is one of the major reasons becoming a partner is so lucrative.

The flip side of this is that new partners must agree to buy out older partners when their day comes. Therefore, any plan for bringing in new partners must include a provision for a partner retirement/buyout plan.

The basis for these buyouts is the clear and substantial value of a CPA firm and the relative ease with which it can be sold to other firms at an attractive price. The main basis for this price is the value of a firm's client base, which for CPA firms, is largely annuity-based. It's considered an intangible value because it's almost never included in the firm's balance sheet. Partner agreements routinely provide for the interest of departed partners to be purchased by the firm to avoid the need to liquidate the practice to generate funds to pay the buyouts.

No, It's Not a Ponzi Scheme

Many new partners, when hearing how partner buyout plans work, fear they sound dangerously close to Ponzi schemes. New partners pay out one partner after another after another, with their own payday feeling like a foggy uncertainly because it's decades away?

While I can see how new partners without any experience operating a CPA firm buyout plan might be a tad apprehensive, let me seek to provide some comfort and show that this fear is greatly exaggerated.

To start with, here are a few statistics from The Rosenberg MAP Survey:

- 94% of all CPA firms with five or more partners have a partner buyout plan. For firms with two to four partners, this percentage is a bit lower: 78%. The main reason the percentage is lower for smaller firms is that, frankly, smaller firm partners' exit strategy is more likely to be selling the firm instead of keeping it independent. Some of these firms don't bother to create a buyout plan that will never be used.

  The point: New partners can take solace in the fact that the vast majority of CPA firms have a buyout plan in place and therefore it is a best practice.

- The vast majority of multipartner firms over $5M in revenue are actually making buyout payments, which shows that the plans work and are affordable. More than four-fifths (82%) of firms with revenue over $10M are making payments. For firms with revenue of $5-10M revenue, 66% are making payments. It's important to understand that if firms are *not* making payments, that simply means that no partners have retired yet under their buyout plan.

- Annual payments to retired partners are very small, 1-2% of revenue. Very affordable.

In addition to the statistical evidence that buyout plans are sound practices, new partners should be comforted knowing that properly written plans have several features that protect the firm's cash flow by limiting any burdens the buyout obligations may cause:

116

- The main way that firms fund the buyouts is by no longer having to compensate the retired partner. In fact, these savings usually *exceed* the buyout payments.

- Most plans have a statutory limit on total annual buyout payments, usually 5-10% of annual revenue. One of the main benefits of this provision is to protect the firm if too many partners retire at the same time.

One final piece of reassurance to new partners: In my 20 years of consulting to CPA firms, I've never heard one firm that found the buyout obligations to be unaffordable. However, it is true that when firms feel their future is uncertain due to impending partner retirements, include-ing situations when too many partners plan to retire at the same time, they usually sell out to address this concern.

Now that we've showed that the buyout plan will not become an onerous obligation, let's look at ways CPA firms customarily operate that should reassure their partners that the buyout plan is viable.

1. Most firms grow every year. Virtually all firms at least retain their revenue level from the prior year.

2. This growth plus other factors often result in firms bringing in new partners every now and then, helping to assure a reasonable spread of partner ages, minimizing the likelihood that too many partners will retire at the same time.

   New partners, along with current partners, need to proactively con-tribute to the firm's efforts to develop staff into future partners. A new partner cannot possibly afford to pay the buyouts of all older partners if he or she is the only one left to make the payments.

3. It's natural to be concerned about the retirement of partners with lifelong, deep client relationships. If the firm's partners have operated as Lone Rangers and very few or even no other firm members have been brought in to serve the clients and forge relationships with them, then the Ponzi fear may be somewhat justified. It is difficult to retain clients after the departure of the main relationship partner.

117

However, even in this worst-case scenario, properly written buyout plans require proactive transition of client relationships for the departed partner to be eligible for buyout payments. If a reasonably decent effort is made at client transition, the vast majority of firms have a very strong client retention rate when partners retire, even when transition efforts are less than expected.

4. The firm has provisions for new partner buy-in and buyout that are conservative and are not onerous.

If all of these ducks are in a row, there is little reason for new partners to fear the buyout plan becoming a Ponzi scheme.

The Buyout Plan: Three Big Issues to Decide

1. Will the buyout be limited to capital only? Or will it include a goodwill provision? (95% of all firms with retirement plans pay both capital and goodwill).

2. How will the goodwill be valued? Should it be 100% of revenue? 90%? 80%? 60%? 40%?

3. How will an *individual* partner's buyout amount be determined?

Goodwill Valuation Rates

There was a time when CPA firms routinely sold for 100% of revenue, and internal buyout plans used the same valuation percentage. But times have changed. For many years now, the average goodwill valuation rate used for partner buyout plans has hovered around 80%. Why the decrease?

CPAs have become more conservative, feeling that the world we live in has become increasingly precarious. The CPA profession in particular faces a never-ending series of challenges such as tax reform, technology reducing compliance work, and the need to replace retiring rainmakers. Valuing goodwill at a lower amount eases the discomfort over the future that younger partners may feel.

With some important exceptions, firms are generally willing to continue paying buyouts to retired partners despite losing some of the retiree's clients. The difference between a 100% and 80% valuation essentially amounts to a bad-debt reserve for client loss.

Even though 80% may be the average, there are still many firms at 100% of fees. There are also many firms well *below* 80%. Virtually all of the Top 100 firms are at 80% or less. Every firm needs to select a goodwill valuation rate the partners are comfortable with. Most firms err on the side of being conservative.

Buyout Best Practices and Key Concepts

1. **The value of a CPA firm is the sum of its capital and goodwill.** The goodwill valuation method is critically important. See the previous paragraphs.

2. **Partner buyouts are a form of deferred compensation.** As compensation, they should be primarily performance-based (perhaps not as much as partner compensation, but close). As with partner compensation, a partner must *earn* the buyout by contributing to the firm's revenues, profitability and overall success. The buyout should *not* be based on non-performance-based methods such as ownership percentage or pay-equal.

   As we will see in a few pages, the two Cadillac systems for computing partners' buyouts are heavily linked to their compensation—which, we hope, is performance-based and therefore a measure of what they contributed to building the value of the firm. If a firm's partner compensation system is *not* performance-based (if it is based on ownership percentage, pay-equal or seniority), then there is great risk that individual partners may receive buyouts in excess of what they deserve or earned, in the eyes of those who will write the buyout checks.

3. **The math must work.** The acid test of a well-conceived, financially viable retirement plan is whether, when a partner retires, the remaining partners earn *more* money (or at least no *less*) than prior to the retirement. The main reason this is possible is that the remaining partners no longer have to compensate the retiring part-

119

ner. If the math works, the money saved on the retiree's compensation will be enough to fund that person's payments, pay the salary of the partner's replacement and perhaps have a little left over to increase the remaining partners' compensation.

If this is not the case, then the plan may not be financially viable.

Let's illustrate an ideal scenario where the math works. Assume the following:

- The retiring partner's compensation is $350,000.
- His or her goodwill-based benefits are $1M over 10 years, or $100,000 per year.
- The firm will hire an experienced staff person, at a compensation level of $150,000, to replace the retiring partner.

Summary of the annual cash flow (or, how the math *works*):

+	Saved compensation of retiring partner	$350,000
-	Retirement benefits	(100,000)
-	Salary/benefits of experienced person	(150,000)
+	Net additional income to remaining partners	$100,000

4. **A partner buyout plan is not a savings plan.** There is a natural tendency to view the firm's partner retirement plan as a personal savings plan, but that's not how these plans work. A savings plan is a pile of money that increases in value over time that can be 100% withdrawn for any reason at any time by the owner.

CPA firm retirement plans are quite different. Designed to encourage partners to stay with the firm for the long haul, they strictly limit departed partners' ability to withdraw benefits if they leave early in their tenure with the firm. There are two reasons for this:

- Retirement within the first 10 to 15 years or so of a partner's tenure with the firm could result in windfall benefits to the individual.

- Partners are very hard to replace. Firms really need to retain their partners over a long period. Often the early departure of even one partner can damage the firm for years to come.

To ensure that a partner buyout plan does not function like a savings plan, CPA firms typically adopt several restrictions on making buyout payments. More on this later.

5. **The plan must have safety valves.** Well-written retirement plans adopt several tactics to make sure the annual payment of all buyout payments will not be a strain on the firm's cash flow:

- The math must work. See item #3 above.

- Vesting conventions are adopted for goodwill (not capital). They require that a departing partner achieve both a certain number of years as a partner and a certain minimum age in order to be 100% vested. When these conditions are not met, payouts are reduced.

- There is an annual limit on all buyout payments as a percentage of the firm's revenues; 5-10% is common.

- The payout term is long enough so that the annual payments are affordable; 10 years is most common.

- No interest is paid on goodwill payments.

- Some firms reduce benefits if the departing partners' clients leave after they retire. This is usually restricted to large clients or services.

- Well-written plans have strict requirements for notice and client transition in order for the retiring partner to receive benefits. If these requirements are not met, then the firm, at its sole discretion, can reduce the benefits.

6. **The plan has provisions for retired partners to continue working, either full-time or part-time.** At least 90% of CPA firm partners want to continue working after their "retirement." They love it so much they can't let go! Firms' partner agreements adopt a wide variety of provisions governing how this works. But the main

requirement should always be this: Regardless of the terms of the post-retirement work arrangement, the partner must provide *value* to the firm in the eyes of the remaining partners. Partners do not have an inalienable right to keep working as long as they want.

7. **Internal vs. external goodwill valuations.** A common perplexity is this: If CPA firms are commonly sold for one times revenue, why should a firm's internal buyout plan use a goodwill valuation well below 100% of revenue? There are three simple answers:

   - Supply and demand. When firms are sold, there are many buyers, so that usually bids up the price. But internally, there is only one buyer, the firm. So that keeps the price lower.

   - Firms have a strong desire to be as conservative as possible. Client retention is usually higher when partners retire than when a firm is acquired. So based on net revenues retained, 100% can equal 80%.

   - The net value retained could be higher when partners retire internally at a lower valuation rate instead of selling the firm to a buyer at a higher valuation (sales) rate. This is due to the fact that client retention is almost always higher when partners retire than when the firm is sold to an outside buyer.

   Here is an example:

Net Value Retained	Sell to Outsider	Sell Internally
Fee Volume of Firm	$700,000	$700,000
Actual Client Retention	60%	95%
Fees Retained	**$420,000**	**$665,000**
Price	100%	80%
Net Buyout	**$420,000**	**$532,000**

   So, as strange as it seems, on a net basis, an 80% valuation can exceed a 100% valuation.

Six Systems Used to Determine Partners' Goodwill Payments

This chart shows the different systems that firms across the country are using. The data is from a recent edition of The Rosenberg MAP Survey.

Six Systems Used to Determine Partners' Goodwill Payments

System	2-4 Partners	5-7 Partners	8-12 Partners	13 + Partners	Total
Multiple of compensation	34%	49%	58%	61%	47%
Book of business	8%	15%	7%	0%	9%
Ownership percentage	25%	16%	4%	4%	15%
Average Annual Value (AAV)	18%	11%	22%	25%	17%
Fixed	13%	9%	7%	7%	10%
Equal	2%	0%	2%	4%	2%

The Two Best Systems

Multiple-of-compensation method. The most common method used by firms, multiple of compensation is quite simple: Goodwill-based retirement benefits of each partner are equal to the person's compensation immediately prior to retirement times a predetermined multiple. Almost all multiples range from 2 to 3.

Here's an example. Assume a firm chooses a multiple of 3. Further assume that a partner's income is $500,000 prior to retirement. Using the multiple-of-compensation method, this partner would receive a goodwill buyout of $1.5M. If payable over ten years, that's $150,000 a year. As a practical matter, most firms average the highest three of the partner's last five years' income, or other similar convention.

AAV method. The letters stand for "average annual value," but these words don't adequately describe the system. A better name would be the "cumulative benefits" method.

The fundamental aspect of this system: New partners are not entitled to any portion of the goodwill value of the firm that was built up *before* they became partners, unless they *purchase* it as part of the buy-in.

Here is an illustration of the AAV method:

Assumptions:
1. The firm has annual fees of $5 million.
2. The firm chooses to value the goodwill at one times fees, which comes to $5 million.
3. There are four partners prior to a fifth partner being admitted.
4. The firm grows at 10% per year.
5. Total partner income is 1/3 of revenue, or $1,667,000.
6. Partner income is allocated as follows for partners A-E, respectively: 30% - 30% - 15% - 15% - 10%.

The AAV Method Illustrated

Ptnr	Balance 1/1/20	Increase in Fees	Balance 12/31/20	Increase in Fees	Balance 12/31/21
A	$1,500,000	$150,000	$1,650,000	$165,000	$1,815,000
B	$1,500,000	$150,000	$1,650,000	$165,000	$1,815,000
C	$1,000,000	$75,000	$1,075,000	$82,500	$1,157,500
D	$1,000,000	$75,000	$1,075,000	$82,500	$1,157,500
New Ptnr E	$0	$50,000	$50,000	$55,000	$105,000
Total	$5,000,000	$500,000	$ 5,500,000	$550,000	$6,050,000

The annual increase in fees is allocated to the partners in the ratio of their income allocation percentages. The AAV system works only if the partner compensation system is *performance-based*. Income is shared based on the ratio of their contributions to the firm's profitability, which should be reflected in the ratio of the partners' respective incomes.

New partners build up their retirement benefits year by year. When a partner retires, the retiree's benefits are re-allocated to the remaining partners. This is the fastest way for newer partners' benefits to jump up.

Partner Buyout Plans:
28 Main Provisions

Terms	What Firms Are Doing
Capital	
1. Total capital defined	Mostly accrual basis capital; some cash basis.
2. Payout period	5-10 years.
3. Interest on payments?	Almost all firms.
4. Individual share determined	Partnership accounting is most common; some owner percentage.
Goodwill	
1. The math must work.	When a partner retires, the other partners' income either increases or at worst, does not go down.
2. Goodwill valuation	80% is average; 100% still common.
3. Determination of individual goodwill amount	• Most use a multiple of comp, say 3 times • Some firms use cumulative growth (AAV) • Smaller number use ownership percent, book of business or pay-equal • Comp system must be performance-based & fair if multiple of comp or AAV method used. • Avoid penalizing preretirement partner for transitioning clients to other partners.
4. Role of firm ownership	Virtually none.
5. Term of payout	10 years is very common, though there are signs of this inching up.
6. Interest on benefits?	Almost never.
7. Vesting	• Many variations. • Many firms base it on age as well as years as a partner. • Most common for full vesting: 10-20 yrs. • Common for reductions in vesting if partner retires prior to age 60-66.

Terms	What Firms Are Doing
	• Common for new partners to wait 5 years to vest *anything*.
8. Age for 100% vesting	Ranges from 60 to 66.
9. When retirement allowed	Most allow it any time. Some firms require the partner to reach a minimum age, say 50, before being eligible for any payments.
10. Notice required	No notice → No goodwill. More and more firms are moving to 2 years.
11. Client transition practices	No transition → No goodwill. If retiree fails to comply with the firm's client transition policy, the firm, at its discretion, can reduce buyout.
12. Retirement mandatory?	Most firms have this at 65 or 66, with provision that if partner wishes to continue working, annual approval is needed.
13. Limits on annual payout	Often 5-10% of revenue.
14. When payments start if partner withdraws	Most will begin payments when a partner withdraws.
15. Funding	Very little except for life insurance.
16. Reduce benefits if clients leave?	• 80% of firms do not reduce; 20% do. • Pegging benefits *below* 1x fees provides reserve for client loss.
17. Nontraditional and/or non-annuity-type services.	Most firms do not pay buyouts if these services walk away when the partner retires. The key: Has the partner institutionalized the services?
18. Retired partners work part time	Common: Pay 40% of time + new business commission; but retiree must provide *value*.
19. Health coverage	Varies but usually stops when partner retires.
20. Taxation of payments	Deductible by firm; regular income to retiree.
21. Death and disability	Most treat it the same as regular retirement.
22. Disability— continuation of partner's comp	Common: until disability policy kicks in or until disability is official. 100-75-50-25 is common. No pay after one year.

Terms	What Firms Are Doing
23. Withdrawing partners	Must pay 100-150% of fees for clients/staff taken.
24. Clawback	If the firm is sold for better terms during the payout period, retired partners benefit from higher terms over a 5-year phase-out period.

12

The CPA Firm Partner Agreement: What Firms Should Address and What Partner Candidates Should Know Before They Sign

What Is a Partner Agreement?

According to nolo.com:

"A partner agreement spells out the rights and responsibilities of the firm's owners. Without one, firms will be ill-equipped to settle or avoid conflicts because if certain key passages are missing or written improperly, the courts will intervene in ways that the partners may not like. A partner agreement allows the firm's partners to structure their business relationships with each other in ways that suit their desires, needs, and preferences."

Any book on partner agreements will have an obligatory paragraph like that. Here is a more in-depth description that may be illuminating.

A partner agreement is a legally binding document that stipulates how the firm will be governed. By signing this agreement, all the partners agree to abide by the document's terms. The partner agreement essentially contains the rules of the game. This helps the firm minimize problems and disputes such as these:

1. One-size-fits-all state laws. In the absence of a signed agreement, state laws, which vary by state, will be used to settle partner disputes. By necessity these state laws are one-size-fits-all rules. It's much better to have an agreement in which the firm's partners specify the rules for their firm *on their own terms*. Examples:

    a. A CPA firm decides *not* to provide for payment of goodwill-based retirement benefits. Without a partner agreement, state law could require the firm to pay these benefits if the departed partner sues the firm for them.

    b. If the founder or a power partner dies or becomes disabled, the other partners may be legally entitled to a much larger share of the firm than they deserve.

2. Voting. Great example: A four-partner firm asked me to help them with their first-ever partner agreement. The firm was dominated by its founder. He brought in most of the firm's clients, managed the firm and was the primary driver of virtually everything in the firm, including its success and profits. Without a written agreement, the founder was susceptible to the three other partners essentially throwing him out of the firm, with or without valid cause.

3. Allocating firm income. Most firms allocate partner income based on partner performance, as opposed to nonperformance methods such as ownership percentage, pay-equal or seniority. Although many firms factor this into the allocation system, in the absence of a written agreement, in the case of a dispute, it's possible a court could force the income to be allocated on ownership percentage rather than performance.

4. Expelling partners. Specify circumstances that allow the firm to expel a partner. Without this, firms may be greatly limited in terminating partners, even for egregious acts.

5.   Other critical issues that partner agreements need to address:
   *   Admission of new partners.

   *   Duties of partners.

   *   Duties and authorities of the managing partner.

When duties and rules of conduct are documented in a partner agreement and signed by all partners, they are more likely to adhere to these rules than if there is nothing in writing.

Critical Provisions in a CPA Firm Partner Agreement

There will be two different types of readers of this chapter, and they will read the text from different perspectives:

1.   **Partners of the firm.** They should read this chapter and ask:

   a.   Is our partner agreement up to date and does it contain the provisions cited in this chapter?

   b.   Does our agreement provide strong protection of the firm and minimize the possibility of disputes among the partners?

   c.   If we expect partners from merged-in firms and new partners promoted from staff to sign our partner agreement, are we proud to show them our document because we know it's current, strong, fair and properly written?

2.   **Partner candidates.** Becoming a partner in the firm is a big deal, something you should be proud of. Part of being a partner is signing the firm's partner agreement. Is the firm's agreement current, coherent, fair and properly written? Are you comfortable with the restrictive provisions and obligations that go along with becoming a partner? Do you understand all the provisions?

Here are those critical partner agreement provisions:

1. **New partner buy-in.** The firm should require this because (a) all owners should have a meaningful amount of money invested in the firm that is at risk and (b) new partners should not be allowed to acquire part of a valuable asset without paying for it. The buy-in should be paid to the firm, not individual partners.

2. **Partner capital.** Addresses how each partner's capital in the firm is accounted for and calculated. Once capital is contributed and built up in the firm, most firms don't allow partners to withdraw it except as routine partner draws and distributions determined by the firm's management.

3. **Ownership percentage.** This provision defines what ownership percentage means. It usually addresses how ownership percentage impacts (a) compensation, (b) buyout, (c) voting and (d) new partner buy-in and (e) how the proceeds of a firm sale are allocated to the partners. As stated earlier in this book, well-managed firms virtually eliminate the impact of ownership percentage on these five factors.

4. **Voting.** Specifies how formal votes are taken, including what actions require a vote. There are two types of votes: Majority votes for most issues and supermajority votes for critical issues such as partner admissions and mergers. The firm's most productive partners will want to ensure that a group of minority owners are unable to band together to stage a coup. The firm's new partners will want to ensure that they are not assigned such a low voting percentage as to disenfranchise them.

5. **Overall firm management.** The main responsibility for managing the firm should rest with a management team, primarily the managing partner and the executive committee. To be effective, the firm's managing partner should not have to take a vote every time a decision must be made. The partner agreement specifies what the MP's duties and authorities are. The agreement also specifies the duties and authorities of an Executive Committee and a Compensation Committee, if the firm has these committees.

6. **Partner compensation.** Many people are surprised to hear that CPA firm partner agreements should be very brief on how partner

income is allocated. One or two sentences at most, using very general terminology, is all that is needed. This is because compensation systems are changed frequently, and the firm doesn't want to have to change the agreement every time it makes a modification.

However, just because the partner agreement is short on verbiage for how partner income is allocated doesn't mean that the system is simple. New partners should thoroughly understand how the system works. Ideally, the firm will have prepared a document or policy that explains how its partner income is allocated.

7. **Partner duties.** Partners must devote 100% of their time to the firm; there should be no side businesses or service to boards without the firm's approval. All income from professional endeavors, even on the side, should go to the firm. Performing effectively as partners is a tough, demanding job requiring long hours; firms don't want their partners distracted by outside pursuits. New partners must read this section carefully because signing the agreement means that they commit to complying with the restrictions. A staffer who aspires to create a burgeoning real estate business on the side will not want to become a partner in a CPA firm.

8. **Partners' outside activities**. Certain outside activities usually require partner approval. They include (a) owning other businesses, actively or passively, (b) investing in clients' businesses, (c) serving as trustees and executors and (d) serving elective civic offices. If you want to become the mayor of your city, this may not be compatible with being a partner.

9. **Prohibitions and expulsion of partners**. If you don't provide for these, the firm may legally be limited in taking disciplinary action, including termination, against partners who commit "bad acts" or fail to meet minimum performance standards. Be specific about the retirement benefits that an expelled partner will not receive.

10. **Nonsolicitation covenant**. The firm must protect its intellectual property and assets. They were developed over many years at considerable expense to the firm; departing partners shouldn't be allowed to simply take these assets for free. If partners leave the firm, they should be prohibited from taking clients, prospects and staff, *even if* they offer to pay for them. If they violate this prohibition, they should be required to pay a significant but not unreasonable

amount of liquidated damages for this offense, regardless of whether the clients, prospects and staff were solicited or not.

11. **Non-equity partners**. For decades, CPA firms erred in promoting managers directly to equity partners as a retention device, regardless of their ability to function as equity partners. Today, 60% of firms provide for a position between manager and equity partner, the non-equity partner. The trend these days is for firms to have fewer equity and more non-equity partners. See the next section of this chapter for details on the non-equity partner position and how it is different from that of equity partners.

12. **Mandatory retirement**. Yes, this is *still* legally applicable to partners in the vast majority of states. Even if the firm wishes to allow partners past retirement age to continue working, it needs a mandatory retirement provision. This way, the *firm,* not the *older partner,* decides if an aging partner whose skills have eroded should be allowed to continue working. This provision is a great way to address the retirement issue for a specific partner.

13. **Death and disability.** These departures from the firm should be treated the same as a normal retirement. In the case of a disability, clear guidelines are needed for compensating the partner while disabled and determining when the person should be declared retired. Disabled partners should not be allowed to be a financial burden on the firm.

14. **Sale of the firm**. Firms have been known to abandon their partner buyout methodology when the firm is sold. An allocation method is needed to distribute the proceeds of the sale. The allocation should be based on each partner's relative retirement benefits.

15. **Partner retirement/buyout.** This was addressed thoroughly in Chapter 11. Firms should either provide for goodwill-based partner benefits or specifically state that there will be none. Agreements that are silent on this may result in a court ruling that departed partners are due for goodwill an amount of money well in excess of what they deserve or have earned.

Reasons for Adding New Equity Partners

We explored the reasons for equity partners in great detail in Chapter 2. Here are the key points:

1. New partners deserve the promotion to such a great extent that the firm can't afford NOT to admit them to the ownership ranks.

2. The firm needs to expand its partner ranks.

3. The firm needs to replace a departed partner.

4. It rewards long-time managers who have solid client service skills.

5. It's part of a succession planning strategy.

6. Partner promotions send a strong message to the staff.

7. It energizes the partner group.

8. It's part of a merger strategy.

Reasons for Adding New Non-Equity Partners

1. Non-equity partner is often a partner-in-training position. The firm recognizes that a manager has the talent and skills to function as a partner. It provides the non-equity position so that both the firm and the partner candidate have an opportunity to work with each other to determine if the individual is a good fit in the firm's equity partner group. At many firms, it's perfectly acceptable to be a permanent non-equity partner.

2. It enables a firm to recognize the stature and contributions of a valuable, long-time staffer who does not meet all the criteria for being a partner (usually bringing in business is lacking).

3. It's a staff retention tactic. Certain long-time staff who are now managers reach the point in their career when they feel that if they don't make partner, or if they can't call themselves "partner" to the outside world, including friends and family, then it's time to move on. Years ago, firms made the mistake of promoting these valuable people directly to equity partner. But firms have been finding that the non-equity position is a good position so that these valuable people can now be called partners.

4. Some firms, usually with just a few partners, have built up their compensation and the firm's value to such a high extent that they simply don't want to share it with others who don't produce at their high level. So people are made non-equity partners and compensated very well, perhaps better than other firms' equity partners.

5. For lateral hires, it provides both sides an opportunity to test each other out before fully committing to an ownership arrangement. The same applies to merged-in partners.

Equity vs. Non-Equity Partners

Characteristic	Non-Equity Partner	Equity Partner
1. Is the person a DRIVER in the firm?	To some degree.	Often.
2. Expected to bring in business?	To some degree. Encouraged but often not required.	Often.
3. Manage a certain size of client base?	Usually several hundred thousand dollars in billings, some of it delegated to NE partner.	Often $1M or more.
4. Work on clients of other equity partners?	Some. Varies from firm to firm.	Very little.
5. Technical skills?	High level. New non-equity partners still may need help.	High enough that a second review is seldom needed.
6. Is staff-level work delegated?	More than as manager but delegation not always possible.	Almost always.
7. Client relationships?	Good relationships but sometimes secondary to equity partner relationship.	Strong relationship. Always the primary partner.
8. Buy-in?	No	Yes
9. Liability?	No	Yes

10. Held out as a "partner"?	Yes	Yes
11. Attends partner meetings?	Yes, but excused when confidential issues discussed.	Yes
12. A vote?	Not legally, but fully allowed to influence others' decisions.	Yes
13. Determination of comp?	Set subjectively by management, just as for a staff.	Fits in with the firm's equity partner comp system.
14. Participate in the firm's profits?	Not directly, but usually eligible for bonus based on NE partner's impact on the firm's overall success, including profitability.	Always.
15. Receive W-2?	Almost always, paid as a salary.	No, unless firm is a corporation.
16. Participate in the firm's retirement benefits?	Rare, but a growing number of firms are beginning to award buyouts to NE partners, albeit at lower amount than equity partners.	Always
17. Access to partner comp data?	Usually not.	Yes, but if a closed comp system, access is limited.
18. Access to confidential data: financials, operating stats, etc.	Usually, but not partner compensation data.	Yes, except certain partner comp data if a closed system.
19. Sign client reports?	Some do; some don't. AICPA ethics says the guideline must be included in the firm's quality control policy.	Yes

13

What Prospective Partners Should Ask Their Firm,

What the Firm Should Ask Prospective Partners

This chapter should be read from the perspective of two different audiences: prospective partners and existing partner groups.

- **Prospective partners.** *Well* before accepting a partnership offer, prospective partners should ask basic, critically important questions to help them judge whether accepting it would be a smart decision.

- **Existing partner group.** *Well* before extending a partnership offer, the firm should get its house in order to avoid being embarrassed by smart questions posed by partner candidates.

Questions Prospective Partners Should Ask Their Firm

It's one thing for a staff person to join a CPA firm, enjoy the job and experience success via nonstop promotions, feeling all along that the firm is a great place to work. But it's quite another thing for a staffer to consider whether or not to accept a partnership offer that may come in the future.

Joining the partner ranks of one's CPA firm is an awesome opportunity that a staffer should be immensely proud of. But prospective partners should approach the offer the same way a company contemplates merging with another organization. They must separate the emotion and euphoria of the partnership opportunity from the need to perform due diligence on the firm to verify that becoming a partner will be a good business decision.

These are the issues that prospective partners should investigate to determine if becoming an owner in the firm is the right choice for them.

1. Does the firm have written criteria for making partner? Are the criteria reasonable? Attainable?

2. What will be your role as a new partner? How will it change from your manager role? Beware if the firm wants you to continue functioning as a staff person, working on the other partners' clients, without being allowed to perform like a partner.

3. Does the firm have a proper partner agreement, spelling out sensitive but critically important provisions such as death and disability, mandatory retirement, partner duties and prohibitions, causes for expulsion, managing partner duties and voting? No one should agree to be an owner in a business without a properly written, current, signed partner agreement in place.

4. How is voting structured? If your ownership percentage is small and voting is based on ownership percentage for all issues, you won't have any say in decisions. Voting should be one person, one vote with simple majority rules. The exceptions are major issues: mergers, changing the partner agreement and a few others, the latter of which should be voted on a supermajority basis.

5. How is partner income allocated?

a. Is the system performance-based or based on non-performance factors such as ownership percentage, pay-equal or seniority? Nonperformance-based systems usually make it difficult for new partners to achieve the income that their performance warrants. Also, in nonperformance-based systems, a few older partners may be paid well in excess of what they are worth, which will restrict the earning power of newer partners.

b. If the firm uses a formula to allocate partner income, does it succumb to common flaws of formulas that could cause the new partners' compensation to be determined unfairly? Here are some common flaws prospective partners should look out for:

   i. Partners hoard billable hours and clients, thus failing to properly delegate and work as a team.

   ii. Partners manipulate or game the formula to do what's best for themselves at the expense of the firm.

   iii. Production data is weighted heavily to the near-exclusion of critically important intangible performance measures such as firm management, staff mentoring, teamwork and loyalty.

   iv. New partners often don't fit into the formula because they haven't built up their client base sufficiently to enjoy opportunities for income increases. If this happens, what will be the impact on the new partner's compensation?

6. What is the profitability of the firm? How are revenues and profits trending? If the firm is stagnant, marginally successful or declining, a prospective partner might want to think twice about joining it.

7. Is there a cluster of older partners whose overlapping retirements could threaten the future viability of the firm? New partners don't want to join the partner ranks only to see the firm sold in a few short years because it can't survive the retirement of several key partners at the same time.

8. What is the buy-in? It should *not* be ownership percentage times the value of the firm, which results in onerous buy-in amounts, often of many hundreds of thousands of dollars. Instead, it should be a relatively nominal, fixed amount, say, $75K to $150K. And the

payments should be spread out over several years so that the new partner does not take home less cash than they did as a manager. However, new partners should not expect these nominal buy-ins to result in an ownership share of the firm that is disproportionate to the buy-in amount.

9. Does the firm have a retirement/buyout plan in place?

   a. If not, the partner agreement should specifically state this instead of being silent on it.

   b. If the firm doesn't have a buyout agreement, why not?

   c. The goodwill valuation should be reasonable: no more than 100% of revenue, preferably closer to 80%, which has become the norm.

   d. Annual payouts to all partners should have limitations that protect the firm's cash flow.

   e. Does the firm have any very large clients (10-20% or more of the firm's revenue) that are likely to leave after the lead partners retire, thereby putting the firm in a position of paying an excessive buyout?

   f. To be eligible to receive buyouts, partners should be required to provide plenty of notice (at least one year, preferably two) and proactive, measurable client transition. Partners should never be allowed to receive their buyout while controlling clients.

10. When partners start retiring and begin receiving their buyouts, how will this impact the income of the remaining partners? The plan should be structured in such a way that the remaining partners earn either (a) *more* income or (b) *no less* than their income before the partner retired. This is made possible by no longer compensating the retiring partner and using those savings to fund the buyout payments.

   Prospective partners should make sure that the firm's buyout plan does not allow partners to begin receiving retirement payments while continuing to totally control their clients.

11. Is there a mandatory retirement policy? You don't want to be a new partner in a firm where old partners work forever or their retirement dates are unclear. Without mandatory retirement, talented

young people won't stay with your firm, and its future viability is in jeopardy.

12. Does the firm have a proper succession planning strategy, in writing? As a young partner who will be obligated to eventually participate in the buyout of all the present partners, you will need to add additional partners as time goes by to perpetuate the firm's leadership and help pay for the buyouts. You don't want to be the last person to turn out the lights.

Questions a CPA Firm Should Ask Prospective Partners

1. Do you want to be a partner?

2. *Why* do you want to be a partner?

3. Do you know what it means to be a partner? Help candidates see:

   a. What the buy-in amount is, why it is asked of new partners and over what period of time they have to pay in.

   b. What ownership percentage means in your firm.

   c. How partner income is allocated. Stress that owners get paid only after all expenses are met.

   d. Voting.

   e. How the partner buyout plan works, including why the firm has a buyout plan.

   f. The partner agreement's key provisions.

   g. The key difference between managing client *relationships* and managing client *work*.

4. Tell the prospective partner: Our partners are aged __ to __. We need a succession plan because we want to stay independent, not merge with a bigger firm. We have two choices:

a. Our preference is to stay independent and pass on the firm to younger partners like you.

b. Merge into a larger firm. If we did this, we would push hard for the firm to hire you and offer you a great future.

What do *you* think of these two options?

5. Share with the manager why it's great to be a partner, financially and professionally.

   a. Higher compensation, perhaps dramatically so.
   b. Building the goodwill value of the firm, which new partners redeem when they retire or leave the firm. This will be a substantial amount.
   c. You're the boss. You're an owner. You get to manage your own business.
   d. You make your own hours.

Ask: Does this sound appealing to you? If it doesn't, what would the package have to include to get you excited about it?

6. How do you feel about being the only owner (if it's going to be a sole practitioner situation)?

7. Do you have any concerns about the risks of owning a CPA firm? What are they?

8. If the manager clearly wants to be a partner, share the firm's financial, production and operational data and metrics. Explain how to interpret this data. Answer questions.

9. Ask: If you are inclined to accept the offer to become a partner, are there important things you would like the firm to train you on? Areas in which you feel inexperienced?

10. What excites you about being a partner at our firm?

11. What else concerns you?

14

Partner Evaluations

Why Firms Do Performance Evaluations of Partners

The classic purposes of a performance evaluation are:

- To improve performance.

- To clarify what is expected of the individual and what is needed to advance.

- To provide management with information to use in making promotion and compensation decisions.

The need for performance evaluations applies to partners as well as staff. Contrary to what many partners may feel, partners *can* and *must* continually improve their performance.

Five Types of Partner Evaluations

These five types of evaluations, taken together, get feedback from all the people a partner works with. The results provide a basis for appraising partner performance.

1. Self-evaluations
2. Staff evaluations of partners
3. Client satisfaction surveys
4. Peer evaluations
5. Evaluations by supervising partners such as the MP and PICs

Let's drill down on each of these.

1. **Self-evaluation.** This can be used in one of two ways: The self-evaluation can be a standalone tool distributed to those participating in the evaluation and income allocation process, such as the managing partner or the compensation committee. Or it can be the start of a traditional performance appraisal by the managing partner or a department head. See the end of this chapter for a great example of a self-evaluation form.

2. **Upward evaluations of the partners by the staff**. The #1 reason staff leave their firm is dissatisfaction with the boss. In a CPA firm, the partners are the bosses. Any firm that is serious about developing excellent staff and being a great place to work must get feedback from the staff on how they see the partners. Upward evaluations help management assess partners' effectiveness with staff. Just as important, they help individual partners understand how they can be more effective at managing staff.

   Many firms are reluctant to conduct upward evaluations. Major reasons for this are that partners fear receiving weak evaluations and don't wish to subject themselves to criticism.

3. Larger firms are more committed to upward evaluations than smaller ones. This list shows what percentage of firms of each size do upward evaluations:

- 72% of firms over $20M

- 44% of firms $10-$20M

- 37% of firms $2-$10M

- Only 3% of firms under $2M

Skeptics of upward evaluations fear that the staff are not mature enough to evaluate partners properly. Here are some reasons:

- When a staff person performs poorly on an engagement and then receives a weak evaluation by the partner, the angry staff person may avenge the poor grade by giving the partner a weak evaluation.

- Some young staff are slow to learn how a professional behaves in a business environment. They may resent a partner's attempts to teach them proper conduct and give the partner a weak evaluation in return.

- Personality differences occur in all walks of life. There are bound to be situations where clashes occur between partners and staff.

- Staff may be reluctant to complete honest evaluations for fear that the partners (their bosses!) will somehow find out who said what. The result could be inflated ratings.

My responses.

- Yes, some staff may give a weak evaluation that is undeserved. The cure is for the firm to be large enough to generate enough evaluations (at least five or six) for *each* partner to minimize the impact of one improper rating. If only two or three evaluations are generated for each partner, it's probably not feasible to conduct upward evaluations.

- I have conducted dozens of upward evaluations. In every one of them, those partners receiving low grades acknowledged the evaluations' validity.

147

- The key to conducting any kind of survey effectively is to use methodology that yields valid results. To get effective upward evaluation results, use the following techniques:

  o Anonymity and confidentiality *must* be guaranteed.

  o To make the staff feel safe to be open and honest in their responses, the survey *must* be tabulated by an outside organization instead of internal personnel.

  o At least 95% participation by the staff is needed.

  o Staff should be allowed to complete evaluations *only* of partners they worked for. No one should be allowed to evaluate a partner based on hearsay from fellow staff.

  o If a partner receives only two or three evaluations, the results should be discarded because the partner may be able to figure out who said what.

4. **Client satisfaction surveys**. These measure clients' satisfaction and loyalty to the firm and identify ways to better serve them. Along with staff, clients are a major group that partners need to interact with effectively.

   Client surveys should do more than determine whether or not clients are happy with the firm's work. They should examine the level of a client's satisfaction and what to do to improve it. In designing a survey, the firm needs to take the time to determine exactly what it needs to know from clients. If you are planning a client survey, consider the following questions:

   - How thorough are we in our approach to your work?

   - How creative are we in our proposed solutions?

   - Do we document our work activities to your liking?

   - Have we responded promptly to your needs?

   - Are you familiar with other services we provide?

   - Would you use us for other services?

   - Are our communications understandable?

- Do we listen well?

- Do we let you know in advance the steps involved in solving your problems?

- Do we anticipate your needs?

- Do we show an interest in you beyond the projects you have engaged us for?

- Has your understanding of the matters we handle for you improved from working with us?

Client surveys can go beyond measuring satisfaction levels. They can be tools for inquiring about clients' needs or interests in additional services your firm offers.

5. **Peer evaluations**. Whereas the first three forms of evaluation are suitable for firms of all sizes, peer evaluations are appropriate only at smaller firms, say, five partners or less. At this smaller size, the partners all know each other well enough to evaluate each other. Once firms get larger than five or so partners, it gets increasingly difficult for partners to evaluate their peers properly. For them, better evaluation options include upward evaluations and reviews by department heads and the MP.

6. **Traditional performance evaluations.** An appraisal session is convened to review the partner's overall performance. The evaluation is performed by a supervising partner such as the MP, PIC or practice group leader. Some firms appoint two partners to jointly conduct this appraisal session. CPA firms below $20M are, unfortunately, not big users of partner evaluations, evidenced in a recent Rosenberg MAP Survey. This list shows what percentage of firms of each size do traditional evaluations:

- 81% of firms over $20M

- 56% of firms $10-$20M

- 35% of firms $2-$10M

- Only 6% of firms under $2M

As with staff, it's useful to have the partner being reviewed complete a self-evaluation form and discuss it with the reviewing partner.

Partner Self-Evaluation and Impact Form

Name_____

Date_____

The firm should provide all partners with key production statistics: their personal billable hours, client base managed, realization on both, age of WIP, age of A/R, etc. Firms don't want people guessing what their actual statistics are.

Many firms use the same form for both partners and managers. The idea is that if firms want their managers to perform and think like partners, they should get used to being evaluated like partners.

1. For your production statistics, summarize the year you had. Explain why the numbers were good (or below expectations or OK, etc.).

   a. Business brought in, net of realization, both from new clients and cross-selling to existing clients.

      _____
      _____
      _____

   b. The size of the client base you managed, net of realization, including retention of clients. Include (a) clients that you transferred to others and that are therefore are no longer on your billing run and (b) clients you managed that appear on other partners' billing runs.

      _____
      _____
      _____

   c. Billable hours, in general.

      _____
      _____
      _____

151

d. Billable hours: Roughly how many of your billable hours could have been done by a staff person? Why did you do them instead of staff?

_____

_____

_____

2. Do the production statistics tell the full story for what you contributed to the firm? If not, give examples of why not. Explain unusual variations from firm standards or goals.

_____

_____

_____

3. Describe your performance in the areas of retaining, developing, mentoring, nurturing and recruiting staff and, in general, helping staff learn and grow. *Be specific.* Explain the extent to which you feel you made a positive impact in these areas and what you did.

_____

_____

_____

a. List separately the names of staff and junior partners who advanced and excelled under your tutelage.

_____

_____

_____

b. If you participated in upward evaluations of yourself by staff, summarize the results. Were you proud of them? Were they fair? What do you plan to do to improve them?

_____

_____

_____

4. To the extent that you have a role in the firm's management and administration, summarize your performance in these areas. Did you meet expectations? Why or why not?

_____

_____

_____

5. Summarize your performance in the following areas:

The technical quality of your work.

_____
_____
_____

Development of new markets, services, specialties.

_____
_____
_____

Engagement management. Includes timely billing of your WIP, optimizing realization, timely collection of your receivables, etc.

_____
_____
_____

Living and breathing the firm's core values; promoting the firm's core values and leading people to live and breathe them too.

_____
_____
_____

6. How *active* were you in business development? What efforts did you make to bring in business for the firm?

_____
_____
_____

7. List your speeches, articles, seminars, and community, civic and charitable activities. How effective were they? What *impact* did they have?

_____
_____
_____

8. Describe your success at *retaining* clients and how you were a *difference maker* to your clients.

_____

_____

_____

9. For your clients, give examples of how you moved services provided to them upscale.

_____

_____

_____

10. Describe the *impact* of your efforts to build a *team* of professionals as opposed to practicing alone like a sole practitioner. Provide evidence of the success of these efforts.

_____

_____

_____

11. For your top five clients, what have you done to ensure that each of them will remain with the firm if you should suddenly leave?

_____

_____

_____

_____

12. For your top five clients, list the names of other firm members who have established meaningful relations (touch points) with the clients, making them "firm" clients rather than "your" clients.

_____

_____

_____

_____

13. List your special accomplishments this year, in areas not previously addressed on this form, that had a meaningful *impact* on the firm.

_____

_____

_____

_____

14. If your partners were asked to cite areas of your performance this past year that need improvement or were disappointing, what do you think they would say about you?

_____
_____
_____
_____

15. Performance of written goals. On a separate sheet, list your goals and indicate the extent to which the goals were accomplished. If the goals were not accomplished, indicate why and give a revised deadline.

16. Use this area to make any additional comments. Include comments necessary for your partners to get a good understanding of the kind of year you had.

_____
_____
_____
_____
_____

15

Final Pearls of Wisdom

"Partner Seniors"

A great episode from an old, award-winning TV show, *M*A*S*H*, is relevant here. The two stars, Hawkeye and Trapper, are captains and doctors serving in the Korean War. They drive to a nearby military base on business. They have brought with them the timid but highly effective company clerk, Corporal Radar O'Reilly. The mischievous captains decide to stop at an officers' club for a drink, but Radar tells them he can't enter because he's not an officer. Hawkeye, ever the schemer, comes up with a solution. He takes one of his captain's bars and pins it on Radar's lapel, and the threesome enter the club.

While they are standing at the bar, sipping their drinks, Radar realizes he is the recipient of an angry stare from a regular army colonel and prays to quickly become invisible. Alas, the colonel confronts Radar and tells him he's not allowed in the bar because he's only a corporal. Hawkeye immediately comes to Radar's defense and politely but author-itatively informs the gullible colonel that Radar is the subject of the army's experimentation with a new rank: a corporal-captain. The skeptical colonel raises his eyebrows, not quite satisfied with Hawkeye's explanation, but decides not to pursue the matter.

One takeaway of this book is that partners, not "partner seniors", should be drivers of their firm. In most cases, firms should refrain from extending partnership offers to smart, capable, valuable, hard-working staff who function fantastically as seniors or managers but lack the leadership skills needed to drive the firm: bringing in business, leading, mentoring staff and inspiring client confidence.

New Partners Need to Be *Impact* Players

An impact player in sports is more than just a productive, loyal member of the team. The team relies on this player to be a consistent winner.

I've always liked this term to describe what a partner in a CPA firm should be. I like it so much that I inserted the term "impact" in the name of the partner self-evaluation form in the previous chapter.

Here are how some thought leaders I've worked with in the CPA profession describe an impact player:

1. "It's critical to see that the hard work it took to earn the partner promotion doesn't stop when one *becomes* a partner. It's just the beginning of a new race. It's the responsibility of new partners to bring up the next generation of partners behind them." (Al Kutchins, founder and co-MP of KRD, Chicago)

2. An impact player keeps the firm relevant. Never accepts the status quo. Is always looking to innovate and willing to change, even if he or she doesn't have a specific management position in the firm.

3. No partner should *ever* take a neutral position on an issue of controversy within the firm. I've always hated surveys that provide people with five-point rating systems with 3 being neutral because people have a natural tendency to be risk averse and give mostly 3s and 4s. But everyone has an opinion on every issue. If you're a partner, you *should*. There is a tendency for new partners to shut up, follow the older partners' lead and not question things. But this is a big mistake. It's the new partners who are in the best place to shake things up. (Paraphrased from Jennifer Wilson of Convergence-Coaching.)

4. CPA firms have a strong tendency to be like most other firms, doing little to differentiate themselves from the competition. Again, it's the new partners who need to attack this lethargy and make their firm stand out.

5. When discussing the promotion to partner with managers, the firm needs to make a compelling case for why it's better to become a partner at the firm instead of starting their own firm. (Angie Grissom, The Rainmaker Companies)

6. "Let new partners lead. Keep them engaged." (Grissom)

7. "If you stay in a nuthouse, you're nuts." (Gale Crosley, Crosley Company). I loved this the first time I heard Gale say it. New partners can't possibly know the inside scoop about the firm's finances, the partners' performance and productivity, their true personalities, the firm's culture, the relationships between the partners and big problems in the firm. Many partners are in for a rude awakening during their first year or two as partner when they learn these things firsthand. My reading of Gale's quote is that if a partner sees that the firm is operating in a dysfunctional manner (the nuthouse), it's up to that partner to do something about it. If the partner does nothing and choose to stay nonetheless, he or she is nuts too, or soon will be.

Announcing and Celebrating a New Partner

When all is said and done, one of the most enjoyable parts of bringing in a new partner is celebrating the occasion. One way firms do this is through making a public announcement that they are admitting a new partner. As a bonus, this doubles as an excellent marketing opportunity for the firm.

New partner announcements should be made to celebrate both non-equity and equity partners. There is rarely mention outside the partner group of a non-equity partner movement to equity partner.

Some tips for making your new partner announcement:

1. Get an updated headshot of the new partner.

2. Gather a list of notable achievements and practice areas the partner works in.

3. Create a written announcement that can be published to your web-site and local news and business journals and distributed to clients. Include the headshot and notable achievements. If the new partner has a practice area the firm wants to promote, all the better.

159

4. Create and share related social media posts.

If the announcements are done properly, they should make readers think, "Wow, this firm is really going places. It continues to develop great new talent, as evidenced by these striking young men and women it has chosen as partners."

In addition to the public announcement, an internal celebration is in order. Firm practices vary widely on this, but you may want to consider:

1. A special internal announcement preceding the external announcement.

2. A party at the office or a more extravagant meal out for selected individuals

3. A meaningful gift to the new partner to acknowledge this milestone achievement.

Partner promotions are a really big deal to all stakeholders: clients, staff, the community, the new partner's family and most of all, to the new partner. The life of a partner at a CPA firm can be pretty humdrum at times. New partner announcements don't happen every day. Use this as a cause for celebration—and maybe a little bragging about the new partner and the firm.

Made in the USA
Columbia, SC
19 November 2020